HOLMES AND THE RIPPER

A Play

Based on the book *Jack the Ripper, the Final Solution* by Stephen Knight

by Brian Clemens

|| SAMUEL FRENCH ||

samuelfrench.co.uk

Copyright © 2002 by Brian Clemens Enterprise Ltd
All Rights Reserved

HOLMES AND THE RIPPER is fully protected under the copyright laws of the British Commonwealth, including Canada, the United States of America, and all other countries of the Copyright Union. All rights, including professional and amateur stage productions, recitation, lecturing, public reading, motion picture, radio broadcasting, television and the rights of translation into foreign languages are strictly reserved.

ISBN 978-0-573-11371-0

www.samuelfrench.co.uk
www.samuelfrench.com

FOR AMATEUR PRODUCTION ENQUIRIES

UNITED KINGDOM AND WORLD
EXCLUDING NORTH AMERICA
plays@samuelfrench.co.uk
020 7255 4302/01

Each title is subject to availability from Samuel French, depending upon country of performance.

CAUTION: Professional and amateur producers are hereby warned that HOLMES AND THE RIPPER is subject to a licensing fee. Publication of this play does not imply availability for performance. Both amateurs and professionals considering a production are strongly advised to apply to the appropriate agent before starting rehearsals, advertising, or booking a theatre. A licensing fee must be paid whether the title is presented for charity or gain and whether or not admission is charged.

The Professional Rights in this play are controlled by Samuel French Ltd, 24-32 Stephenson Way, London NW1 2HD.

No one shall make any changes in this title for the purpose of production. No part of this book may be reproduced, stored in a retrieval system, or transmitted in any form, by any means, now known or yet to be invented, including mechanical, electronic, photocopying, recording, videotaping, or otherwise, without the prior written permission of the publisher. No one shall upload this title, or part of this title, to any social media websites.

The right of Brian Clemens to be identified as author of this work has been asserted in accordance with Section 77 of the Copyright, Designs and Patents Act 1988.

THINKING ABOUT PERFORMING A SHOW?

There are thousands of plays and musicals available to perform from Samuel French right now, and applying for a licence is easier and more affordable than you might think

---

From classic plays to brand new musicals, from monologues to epic dramas, there are shows for everyone.

Plays and musicals are protected by copyright law so if you want to perform them, the first thing you'll need is a licence. This simple process helps support the playwright by ensuring they get paid for their work, and means that you'll have the documents you need to stage the show in public.

Not all our shows are available to perform all the time, so it's important to check and apply for a licence before you start rehearsals or commit to doing the show.

LEARN MORE & FIND THOUSANDS OF SHOWS

Browse our full range of plays and musicals and find out more about how to license a show

www.samuelfrench.co.uk/perform

Talk to the friendly experts in our Licensing team for advice on choosing a show, and help with licensing

plays@samuelfrench.co.uk   020 7387 9373

Acting Editions
BORN TO PERFORM

Playscripts designed from the ground up to work the way you do in rehearsal, performance and study

---

Larger, clearer text for easier reading

Wider margins for notes

Performance features such as character and props lists, sound and lighting cues, and more

---

+ CHOOSE A SIZE AND STYLE TO SUIT YOU

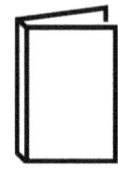 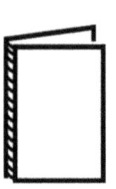 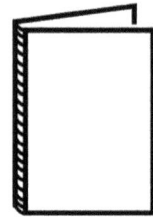

STANDARD EDITION	SPIRAL-BOUND EDITION	LARGE EDITION
Our regular paperback book at our regular size	The same size as the Standard Edition, but with a sturdy, easy-to-fold, easy-to-hold spiral-bound spine	A4 size and spiral bound, with larger text and a blank page for notes opposite every page of text. Perfect for technical and directing use

| LEARN MORE | samuelfrench.co.uk/actingeditions

**Other plays by BRIAN CLEMENS
published by Samuel French**

Anybody for Murder

The Devil at Midnight

The Edge of Darkness

Inside Job

Murder Weapon

Shock!

A Sting in the Tale

Strictly Murder

Will You Still Love Me in the Morning?

Without Trace

FIND PERFECT PLAYS TO PERFORM AT
www.samuelfrench.co.uk/perform

Holmes & The Ripper Cast List:

Opened on the 7th June 1988 at the Grand Theatre, Swansea.

CHARACTERS (in order of appearance):

Sir William Gull – Peter Miles
Catherine Eddowes – Barbara Darnley
John Netley – Sebastian Abineri
Sherlock Holmes – Francis Matthews
Anderson – Roy Purcell
Catherine Mead – Angela Scoular
Policeman – Michael Charlesworth
Dr Watson – Frank Windsor
The Stranger – Jonathan Drysdale
Mrs Hudson – Elisabeth Wade
Potter – Michael Charlesworth
Saunders – Barry J Gordon
Bradbury – Jonathan Drysdale
Mary Kelly – Nicola Warren
Maisie – Janine Russell
Annie Crooks – Barbara Darnley
Lord Salisbury – Barry J Gordon

Presented by John Newman for Newpalm Productions and Mark Furness Ltd with Dina and Alexander E. Racolin and Martin Birrane.

Directed by John David
Designed by Alan Miller-Bunford
Lighting designed by John A. Williams

Sherlock Holmes & The Ripper Murders Cast List:

Opened on the 24th June 2015 at The Haymarket theatre in Basingstoke before regional tour ending at The Blackpool Grand theatre on the 7th November.

CHARACTERS (in order of appearance):

Sir William Gull – Andrew Paul
Lamplighter – Matthew Zilch
Catherine Eddowes – Katy Dean
John Netley – Michael Kirk
Sherlock Holmes – Samuel Clemens
Anderson – Neil Roberts
Catherine Mead – Lara Lemon
Policeman – Matthew Zilch
Dr Watson – George Telfer
The Stranger – Ewan Goddard
Mrs Hudson – Kim Taylforth
Potter – Matthew Zilch
Saunders – Greg Fitch
Bradbury – Ewan Goddard
Drunk – Matthew Zilch
Mary Kelly – Kim Taylforth
Annie Crooks – Katy Dean
Maisie – Katy Dean
Lord Salisbury – Greg Fitch

Directed by Patric Kearns
Designed by Geoff Gilder
Lighting designed by David North

AUTHOR'S NOTES

Sherlock Holmes was a glorious fiction – Jack the Ripper a ghastly fact. To combine the two I have, of course, had to take poetic licence. **Nevertheless the intrinsic facts and details of this story are true.**

Notes to Producer/Director/Designer

This play is conceived as a stylised production and, although I am quite sure and specific as to what the **"sets"** should look like, and have sometimes indicated how this might be achieved, it must ultimately depend upon the expertise and whims of the director and his or her designer.

Similarly with **casting**. At this time I have not allowed logistics to cramp creation but I have indicated where certain roles might be doubled up by one or another artiste, but naturally this is flexible and again, ultimately, in the hands of the director.

Accents. Although one would expect the East End to ring with the sound of Cockney, I have chosen, in the main, not to lapse into the phoentic vernacular, because not only is it tiresome to read (and write!) but it is inaccurate. The East End with its dockside traditions was, and is, a melting pot for many cultures and accents. One would find Glaswegian vying with Geordie, Mancunian etc – and particularly amongst the prostitutes, many of whom came to London from elsewhere to seek a "better" more lucrative life. This is particularly useful and should be borne in mind by those artistes in this piece who are perhaps playing two or more roles, and need to accentuate disparity between them.

Finally, if, in production, you find some of the speeches too verbose, I am not unwilling for **cuts** to be made, so long as the intention remains. The same goes for production. Sherlock Holmes' first entrance, for instance, includes a young man and a woman. These characters could be eliminated should they stretch your resources too far. I only ask that such changes be as a result of production strictures and that they should be carefully considered, and carried out in a thoughtful manner.

Brian Clemens

CHARACTERS

(in order of appearance)

SIR WILLIAM GULL
LAMPLIGHTER
CATHERINE EDDOWES
NETLEY
SHERLOCK HOLMES
YOUNG MAN
YOUNG WOMAN
ANDERSON
KATE MEAD
POLICEMAN
DR WATSON
THE STRANGER
MRS HUDSON
POTTER
SAUNDERS
BRADBURY
DRUNK
MARY KELLY
ANNIE CROOKS
LORD SALISBURY

This named cast of twenty (M14, F6) can be reduced to M8, F3 as under:

1. SHERLOCK HOLMES
2. DR WATSON
3. KATE MEAD
4. CATHERINE EDOWES / ANNIE CROOKS
5. NETLEY
6. SIR WILLIAM GULL /DRUNK
7. ANDERSON / POTTER
8. THE STRANGER / BRADBURY
9. MRS HUDSON / MARY KELLY (provided a dummy is used for Kelly's body) YOUNG WOMAN
10. SALISBURY / LAMPLIGHTER / POLICEMAN
11. SAUNDERS / YOUNG MAN / POLICEMAN (possibly)

The events take place in Mr Holmes' Baker Street rooms and in various other places in and around London in the year 1888 during the reign of Queen Victoria.

ACT I

Curtain rises on:

A stage that is dark save for the spotlit figure of GULL. *He stands upstage on a high platform – and is perhaps under an arch – tall, imposing, like a high priest. He wears the full regalia of a Grand Master Mason of a very high degree. If there is an arch, it bears Masonic symbols. The image should be sinister, almost cabbalistic.*

It is not important, or even desirable, that we fully see or recognise GULL *at this juncture, and if his regalia and/or the lighting shield his face, then so much the better.*

GULL And so, brethren, it came to pass that the Apprentices, Jubela, Jubelo and Jubelum, having brutally murdered the Grand Master Hiram Abiff, took flight. They sought to hide from the authorities of the day, and in this they were successful, but they could not hide from their diligent brethren, and were soon discovered and taken by the shore at Joppa, and there vengeance was exacted; their throats were cut, their breasts ripped open, their hearts and vitals taken out and thrown away to wither to dust and be dispersed by the four winds over land and sea. Thus the spilling of blood was avenged by the spilling of blood, uniting in the act – Fidelity, Fidelity, Fidelity...

With each "Fidelity", GULL *ceremoniously smites the apron he wears, setting the regalia attached there to rattling and jingling.*

The spotlight illuminating GULL *is extinguished, and momentarily the stage is again in darkness. The jingle of* GULL*'s regalia becomes – sound effects – the rattle of an* *approaching hansom cab and, as the scene progresses, we might also introduce the sound of a far off barrel organ, and/or other sounds to bring the atmosphere of Victorian London.*

Downstage, a Victorian gas/street lamp glows brighter and brighter so as to eventually illuminate the **LAMPLIGHTER** *who stands beneath it, using his long pole to ignite and regulate it. (**Note**: the street lamp need not be free standing; it might either be suspended, or giving the impression of being attached to a bracket projecting from the wings).*

As the stage grows brighter we reveal a Street in the East End in 1888. Upstage there is a "flat" suggesting a wall, or part of a building; certainly some part of those mean streets – and beyond it a backcloth, onto which is projected the silhouetted shadow of a hansom cab, entering the area, to stop just the other side of the "flat".

LAMPLIGHTER *shoulders his pole and moves as though to exit, but en route he almost collides with* **EDDOWES** *as she enters. She is a shabby, slightly drunk, prostitute.*

EDDOWES 'Ere! Watch where you're going!

LAMPLIGHTER Better watch where *you're* going more likely. They ain't caught him yet, you know, and he do like to carve 'em. Frippett like you. Yes, he do like to carve 'em.

EDDOWES *(moves to stand under the lamplight.)* You give me a nice bright light, didn't you? Nothing going to happen under a nice bright light. I ain't scared. Anyway, I got to pay the rent, haven't I?

LAMPLIGHTER He do like to carve 'em. You should be home in bed.

EDDOWES What do you think I'm standing here for?

LAMPLIGHTER *exits.* **EDDOWES'** *assumed courage wanes a little, but then she produces a little bottle, takes a swig, feels better for it, and even primps herself, ready for a customer who might happen along.*

During this **NETLEY** *enters from behind the "flat", to stand in the shadows, very still, watching; a curiously menacing figure.*

EDDOWES *has another swig of Dutch courage, and then gags on it as she becomes aware of* **NETLEY**.

EDDOWES Who's that? Who are you?

NETLEY *steps forward into the light.*

NETLEY You can call me "Jack".

EDDOWES Jack...!

She takes a step backwards, and as she does so, **NETLEY** *comes prancing down towards her, holding a bottle of gin; his cheery, drunken grin dispels all her fear.*

NETLEY Jack-the-lad! All the way from Camden Town, with a few bob in his pocket, a gleam in his eye, and a bottle of gin to share.

EDDOWES Here...!

NETLEY C'mon, girl, have a swig of the real stuff. *(She still hesitates)* Your name *is* Kelly, isn't it?

EDDOWES It might be. Then again it might not. What if it is?

NETLEY They told me.

EDDOWES Who?

NETLEY Them... *(He gestures vaguely behind him)* ...back at the pub there. "Mary Kelly" they said, if it's a good time you're after. And that's what I *am* after. A good time.

EDDOWES Yes? And what's your idea of a good time?

NETLEY Depends.

EDDOWES Nothing... "unusual" ...?

NETLEY I'll tell you...a good time...? It's a pork pie in this hand, glass of ale in the other...and an invitation to my mother-in-law's funeral on the mantelpiece!

Thoroughly at ease now, **EDDOWES** *joins in his laughter.*

NETLEY *(cont)* Where'll we go then?

EDDOWES It'll cost you.

NETLEY Never knew a pleasure that didn't.

EDDOWES It'll be a shilling.

NETLEY Bloody hell, you must be good. Aw! But what the heck?! What do they say? "In for a penny, in for a pound"? Well, I ain't got a pound, but I'll be in for a shilling, that I will. Where to?

EDDOWES I got a place down the yard there.

NETLEY C'mon and I'll drive you there in style, I will.

EDDOWES Drive me?

NETLEY I've got my cab, haven't I? *(He bows elaborately)* Your carriage awaits. (**EDDOWES** *laughs)* Come to that, I've got soft leather seats, and a travelling rug, and good springs to take the strain...you ever done it in a cab before?

NETLEY *is leading her away now – and she is willingly going along with him.*

EDDOWES No, but my tea leaves this morning said I was in for a new and exciting experience...!

NETLEY *(handing her the bottle)* Can I trust you with the gin?

EDDOWES You could trust me with the Crown Jewels. But not with gin!

EDDOWES and NETLEY exit behind the "flat". If possible we hear the sound of a cab door opening, the creak of the cab's springs, then we hear EDDOWES laugh, a laugh that quickly becomes a whimper of fear – then she screams – but the scream is almost instantly stifled. Then silence.

Blackout.

Then we hear an orchestra playing a polka of the period, and, slowly the lights come up to illuminate:

The Terrace and Garden.

A grand terrace stands a few feet above, and with some steps running down to the garden beyond (suggested by a close-by shrub, and darkness beyond). Rising from the balustrade is a globe light. This, and the french doors at the back of the terrace, are the main illumination. The french doors are partially draped, and beyond we hear the muted sounds of the orchestra playing for the grand ball that is taking place within. We see the occasional shadow and/or the glimpse of a swirl of skirt, a dancing couple from time to time.

A moment, and then **SHERLOCK HOLMES** *enters through french doors. As he does so, it would be desirable if the sound of the orchestra could be raised louder, then become muted again as he closes the doors behind him.*

He wears full dinner suit of the period – and perhaps sports an honour accorded him once upon a time by a grateful crowned head of Europe. There is a small tension about him. He looks almost furtive as he moves to a darker area of the terrace, glances around, then starts to take something out of his pocket, but stops as **YOUNG MAN** *and* **YOUNG WOMAN** *enter from garden area. Both wear evening dress of the period. He is pursuing her as she hurries back towards the french doors.*

YOUNG WOMAN No, Archie, it's too cold out here.

YOUNG MAN Oh, I say.

YOUNG WOMAN Much too cold. I'm absolutely freezing.

YOUNG WOMAN exits through french doors – **YOUNG MAN** *follows.*

HOLMES *(ironic)* The hot fevered passion of youth.

As he speaks he removes his jacket. Then folds it over the balustrade, pushes up his immaculate shirt sleeve and pulls his bow tie undone. He then uses the tie as a tourniquet around his forearm, holding it tight with his teeth as he produces a hypodermic syringe and proceeds to give himself a fix.

During this action the orchestra within stops playing for a while, so that **HOLMES**, *his "fix" taken, and now pushing down his sleeve again and reaching for his jacket, is unaware of the french doors opening and* **ANDERSON** *entering, to stand, watching* **HOLMES**.

Note: **ANDERSON** *arrives at the tail end of the "fix", just as* **HOLMES** *is pushing the sleeve down, pocketing the hypodermic, and now moving to pick up and shrug on his jacket again, and beginning to tie his tie again. It is as he does this that he becomes aware of* **ANDERSON** *watching him. He is a bit startled but quickly "covers" and regains his normal cool composure.*

ANDERSON I know it is a trifle warm in there, Holmes, but this seems rather extreme.

HOLMES Cold night air can be bracing. *(He breathes deep – the drug taking its effect)* Yes, I feel better already.

ANDERSON You know I could arrest you for what I've just seen.

HOLMES Of course! Congratulations are in order, Sir Robert. It is *Assistant Commissioner* Anderson now, is it not? Arrest me? Arrest a man for taking his prescribed medication?

ANDERSON You have such a document?

HOLMES I know a doctor whom I'm sure would oblige. But don't look so crestfallen, my dear Anderson, there is surely crime enough in London to occupy you at the moment? The protestors in Trafalgar Square...?

ANDERSON *(interjects)* Protestors? Anarchists! Mad dogs!

HOLMES Which is the way your people dealt with them I understand. I read that a man was killed, and more than a hundred injured.

ANDERSON They rioted...! A wild mob...

HOLMES *(corrects) People.* Out of work, hungry...

ANDERSON *(overrides)* They raised their hands against Authority...

HOLMES Empty hands, Brother Anderson. Whereas your men were armed, and mounted, and they rode them down.

ANDERSON For Heaven's sake, man, they spoke out against the Queen – against the Monarchy! You can surely find no sympathy for them?

HOLMES Their method of protest was misguided, but then they had no guide, merely a frustrated anger at how things are, and a hazy vision of what they might be. I cannot totally condemn them when they display such a healthy contempt for some aspects of our society for which I think change is long overdue.

Then, the thoughtful mood giving way again to the playfully teasing one:

Then of course there are the Ripper murders. They must be giving you some sleepless nights? Brutal, barbaric, and yet there is a fascination that I...

ANDERSON *(interjects)* You would not interest yourself in the Ripper Murders, would you, Holmes?

His tone is such that HOLMES *regards him, puzzled.*

HOLMES Are you inviting me? Or warning me?

ANDERSON *(quickly)* No, no, of course not. Naturally. But they are, as you say, barbaric, the work of a deranged mind, not the esoteric kind of crime that *you* are used to investigating...

HOLMES *(interjects)* They are unsolved. Baffling. *Exactly* my kind of crime. I have an ego, you know, and a reputation. And both massaged by success.

ANDERSON Your interference would not be tolerated.

HOLMES You *were* warning me. "Interference"? Others might say "experience".

ANDERSON Perhaps I expressed it too strongly. We are under intolerable pressure – the popular press, the Prime Minister, Her Majesty the Queen herself...and the investigation is at a most delicate stage just now – to bring in an outsider, who might disturb the balance...? We should not be at loggerheads, Holmes. Here, tonight, on such an occasion? Brothers should not be quarrelling.

HOLMES Were we quarrelling?

ANDERSON Nevertheless, I apologise.

He produces a case of cigars, offering them to HOLMES.

Cigar?

HOLMES Thank you, no, I prefer a pipe.

ANDERSON But it would ruin the set of your jacket, eh?

HOLMES My... "medication" serves as an admirable alternative.

ANDERSON Was surprised to see you here at all, Holmes.

HOLMES *regards him questioningly.*

Haven't seen you in lodge for several years.

HOLMES Unavoidable I'm afraid, but I keep faith... *(He presses his hand to his heart)* ...here.

ANDERSON To top it all you turn up at our Ladies' Festival – without a lady.

HOLMES The Worshipful Master is an old friend – and most persuasive.

ANDERSON But surely, amongst your friends there is some lady you might have brought along?

HOLMES There is a lady I might have brought, yes, there was a lady once. We – I – lost touch.

ANDERSON Pity. Isn't just success that massages the ego, you know.

During these last few speeches the orchestra has struck up again behind the french doors.

Well...must go and do my duty by *my* good lady. *(Extends hand)* Brother Holmes.

They shake hands, **ANDERSON** *exits through french doors.* **HOLMES** *remains a moment, adjusting his newly tied tie, and is about to exit, when:*

KATE *(offstage)* Mr Holmes?

It is so soft a whisper that **HOLMES** *is not sure he heard it. He turns and sees* **KATHERINE MEAD** *enter from the darkness of the garden area, to remain just below the balustrade, a slim figure, muffled by the cape and hood she wears.*

Mr Holmes?

KATE *hurries up the steps onto the terrace.*

May I speak with you?

HOLMES I would seem to have no choice, madam.

KATE *pushes back her hood to reveal her pale, but delicately beautiful, face.*

KATE Forgive me, I wouldn't bother you like this unless it were desperately urgent...

HOLMES May I ask your name?

KATE Mead. Mrs Katherine Mead.

HOLMES Mrs Mead, it is usual for those who wish to consult me to come to my rooms in Baker Street and...

KATE *(interjects)* There wasn't time. Anyway, this concerns Baker Street. You must return there immediately, there is not a moment to lose or you will miss him altogether...

HOLMES Miss whom?

KATE The man who is coming there to see you.

HOLMES What man?

KATE I don't know. His face was not clear...

HOLMES Mrs Mead... *(He stops, regards her)* Kate Mead? *(She regards him)* The clairvoyant?

KATE I have been called that, yes.

HOLMES You have also been called "charlatan", "fake", "quack", depending upon which paper one reads.

KATE Mr Holmes...

HOLMES *(overrides)* And I am to return to Baker Street immediately. To meet a man. And for what purpose? To avert a catastrophe? Fire? Flood? The overthrow of the Empire?

KATE It has to do with murder. *(Then, as though the thought just came to her:)* And injustice! Solving murders, bringing justice, isn't that what you are famed for?

HOLMES I suppose it all came to you in a dream...?

KATE No. I am rarely asleep when it happens...

HOLMES A vision then. But it does not extend to the name or the face of this mysterious man soon to visit me.

KATE His face is not clear... No, it is concealed! Bandages, he is swathed in bandages.

HOLMES An injured man?

KATE No! Not injured...he has been hurt, yes, and badly done by, but not injured – please, go now...!

HOLMES Mrs Mead...

KATE *(overrides)* Mr Holmes, you are the one man I would expect to at least keep an open mind. If no man appears then I *am* wrong, I am the charlatan I have been branded, but give me the benefit of the doubt. I know it is important, *I know it*. I beg you to leave now.

HOLMES *regards her, then:*

Give me your hand.

As she speaks, she reaches out to take and hold **HOLMES'** *hand, and then:*

A woman is in your thoughts tonight. A very beautiful woman, tall and slim, and at her breast she wears a cross... no, it is not a cross, it is like...two speckled bands – two snakes entwined! Her hair is red, the colour of...

HOLMES *(softly interjects)* ...autumn's leaves, under the first, pale, morning sun... *(And suddenly he jerks his hand free and:)* I've read many accounts of you, Madam, but none said "witch"!

KATE Please, Mr Holmes, you are wasting time. The man will not stay long, he will be taken away.

HOLMES Taken away? By whom?

At this moment **GULL** *enters through french doors, happy and a little drunk.* **KATE,** *an involuntary move, presses back into the shadows as:*

GULL Ah, Holmes – looking for Brother Anderson.

HOLMES I think you'll find him in the smoking room, Sir William.

GULL Was here, was he? And left with a cigar in his hand, I'll wager. How's *that* for deduction? Eh? *Eh?* Elementary, my dear Holmes, elementary.

GULL exits through french doors again. KATE *moves out of the shadows to gaze after him, pulling her cape tighter around herself as:*

KATE Who was that?

HOLMES His name's Gull. Why will this mysterious man be taken away?

KATE I've told you all I know.

HOLMES But it concerns a murder?

KATE He's a doctor, isn't he?

HOLMES Eh?

KATE That man.

HOLMES Very good. A surgeon actually. Physician to the court.

KATE *(abruptly turns to face him)* Not murder, Mr Holmes. Murders. You *will* go?

HOLMES As far as the occult is concerned I am not a complete sceptic. Nevertheless...yes, against my better judgement, and feeling somewhat foolish, I will go.

Blackout (and during blackout, probably move the terrace)

Almost immediately an area down stage is spotlit, and a moment later a POLICEMAN *enters to run in and stop under the light. He looks shaken, and holds a heavily bloodstained item of* EDDOWE's *clothing. He pulls his*

ACT I

whistle – blasts out on it – and as he moves to exit, still blowing on the whistle:

NEWS SELLER *(offstage)* Murder. 'Orrible bloody murder. Ripper strikes again. Read all about it.

Lights go on to reveal: HOLMES' *chambers. There is an open window, chairs, a desk, doors to hallway and to another area.*

DOCTOR WATSON *is seated deeply in a chair, reading* The Times.

HOLMES *enters.*

WATSON Aha, I was right! Thought you wouldn't see that shindig through to the end. Knew you'd be back early – had a premonition.

HOLMES Now don't you start!

WATSON Eh?

HOLMES Have there been any callers?

WATSON No.

HOLMES Messages?

WATSON Yes, Mrs Hudson. She's popped around the corner to see a neighbour who's a bit poorly. Taken some soup – a proper ministering angel our Mrs Hudson, though charity doesn't begin at home, more's the pity. Soup smelled delicious. But she didn't offer me any.

HOLMES You have been here at least an hour then, probably longer?

WATSON How on earth...?

HOLMES "The soup smelled delicious", and you were here to observe it depart to another destination. Yet as I came through the lower hallway, I smelled nothing, and we both of us know how the pervading aromas of Mrs Hudson's soups linger and tantalise. No, a Hudson soup has not passed this way within the past hour. And during that time, had there been a knock you would have heard...yes, you have been awake the whole time.

WATSON *(challenging)* I might not have been. I might have dozed off.

Then, as he sees HOLMES *looking at the ashtray:*

The remains of my Havana account for only half that time.

HOLMES It is simpler than that, Watson – pages six, seven and eight of *The Times*. A controversial reappraisal of the Afghanistan Campaign, written by a man who was not there...and read by a man who was. Bound to fill you with irritation, if not anger – and the flush of your cheek suggests it was the latter. You have hardly been in the frame of mind to doze.

WATSON Amazing. And absolutely correct in every detail.

HOLMES Would you expect otherwise of me, Watson?

WATSON Been here about an hour and a half. *Wide awake*. You expecting someone?

HOLMES Possibly.

WATSON Someone I know?

HOLMES I doubt it. I doubt it's someone *I* know either.

WATSON *(chuckles)* I see. *(Slight pause)* No, I don't! All right, I give up. *(*HOLMES *regards him)* It's a riddle.

HOLMES It's a riddle to me too, Watson.

WATSON Aha, suddenly all is clear.

HOLMES It is?

WATSON Why you're home so early. I've heard these affairs of yours do one proud at the festive board. Glass or three too many brandies, eh?

HOLMES If I had, it would at least provide some excuse for my behaviour.

WATSON Huh?

HOLMES Rushing home at breakneck speed – chasing a...a hallucination.

WATSON I'm not sure at all that I know what you're talking about.

HOLMES Then that makes two of us. Watson, you see before you a gullible, idiotic, dyed in the wool.

) **HOLMES** *stops short, as, offstage, we hear the door bell jangle. A moment – then the bell jangles again – urgently.* **HOLMES** *and* **WATSON** *regard each other.*

WATSON Mrs Hudson has her key.

HOLMES Go and see who it is, there's a good chap. And if it should happen to be a bandaged man, ask him what kept him, and bring him straight up!

WATSON I say, Holmes, you will eventually let me know what the devil is going on, won't you?

HOLMES Just as soon as I know, my dear Watson.

A baffled **WATSON** *exits.*

(softly) As soon as I know.

NEWS SELLER *(offstage)* 'Orrible bloody murder. Ripper strikes twice in one night. Ripper strikes again. Read all about it.

HOLMES *crosses to the window – closes it, and sound with it.*

As he does so, **WATSON** *enters with* **EDDY – THE STRANGER**.

HOLMES *turns and reacts to* **EDDY**.

> **Note**: It is important that we accept that Holmes, who must have seen pictures of **EDDY**, does not recognise him; at the same time one must not get an unwanted laugh from **EDDY**'s appearance, which, I suggest is as follows:
>
> His entire head is bandaged, a bandage that might extend to his nose, leaving only his mouth and lower face visible. Or – his entire head is bandaged, and might extend to cover one eye; the remainder of his face sports a scrubby beard. He is emaciated, hollow eyed, but his body is youthful. His clothes are of good quality, but are presently tousled, grubby, uncared for. His voice is cultured, but it soon becomes clear that he is under extreme mental stress; thoughts come and go, lucidity mixed with confusion and an inability to remember. He is shaking, agitated – and frightened.

EDDY Draw the curtains!

WATSON Now, look here...

HOLMES *(overrides)* No, it's all right, Watson.

> **HOLMES** *draws the curtains, turns to regard* **EDDY**, *who stares at him, and then, the tension draining away, he starts to sway and stagger.* **WATSON** *and* **HOLMES** *quickly move to support him and sit him in a chair.*

WATSON He's shaking like a leaf.

HOLMES Fetch the brandy.

WATSON May not be advisable, man has a head injury.

HOLMES No, it is not an injury per se.

WATSON Eh?

HOLMES Look at his eyes – there seems to be no sign of a recent concussion. Correct me if I'm wrong.

WATSON No, it would appear so.

HOLMES *(soft)* So she was correct in yet another detail.

ACT I

WATSON Eh?

HOLMES The brandy, Watson. I think we would all benefit from one.

WATSON Ah, yes.

And with alacrity now, he moves to pour brandies. As:

HOLMES Where are you from?

EDDY I...I'm not sure...a long way...

HOLMES How did you get here?

EDDY I walked...ran...then...I took an omnibus. Yes. But they put me off...because I had no money. I...I never carry money.

WATSON Just like our dear Queen, eh?

EDDY Queen?

WATSON Her Majesty, Queen Victoria. I say, the chap's not some awful foreigner, is he? If so, he speaks the Queen's English remarkably well. *(Comes up with a satisfactory explanation)* Probably went to one of our better schools.

HOLMES Watson, he is not deaf, nor is he absent. You may address him directly.

WATSON Yes, yes, quite so.

He hands out the brandies – quaffs one himself.

Best form of address I can think of.

EDDY *drinks, and it seems to calm him.*

Jolly good cognac this.

HOLMES The work of some awful foreigner. Now, sir, what is your name?

EDDY I...have no name.

HOLMES Come now...

EDDY I don't remember! They took my name. They...took it away... *(As he says this, he grips his bandaged head)*

WATSON What on earth's he mean? "Took his name". Somebody stole it, did they? Popped it in a bag and run off with it?!

EDDY *(overrides)* You must not ask my name, and I dare not speak it. It's too dangerous...then they would have to kill Annie – and perhaps you too.

WATSON Really, Holmes, this is getting more and more preposterous...

HOLMES *(overrides)* Who might kill you? Who terrifies you so much...?

EDDY stares at him – struggling with his inner self.

We want to help you. *(Very gently)* Tell me. Put a name to *him* at least.

EDDY hesitates, then, just as it seems he might be about to speak, there is a tap at the door. **EDDY** *is instantly terrified again, on his feet, staring at the door.*

HOLMES *quickly picks up revolver from his desk and:*

Who's there?

MRS HUDSON *(offstage)* It's me, sir...Mrs Hudson.

HOLMES *relaxes, a bit abashed at his alarm. The door opens and* **MRS HUDSON** *enters.*

Just thought I'd let you know I'm back again, sir. And would there be anything you might require? Perhaps some hot chocolate?

HOLMES No thank you, Mrs Hudson.

She pointedly regards the glasses of brandy.

MRS HUDSON Much better for you than hard liquor at this time of night.

HOLMES Thank you, that will be all.

MRS HUDSON Very good, sir. *(Then, as she is about to withdraw, she looks at* **WATSON***)* A *doctor* should know that.

HUDSON *exits.* **HOLMES** *again turns to* **EDDY***.*

HOLMES Now, sir...

EDDY This is indeed a most excellent cognac. I would hazard an oak casked Napoleon.

He has undergone a complete change of manner – we are briefly seeing the real **EDDY** *as:*

Sherlock Holmes. Your name has often come up, one has followed your famous exploits with a keen interest. Personally we feel that the gratitude of the nation is long overdue. A knighthood. But you have enemies, jealous rivals.

Suddenly, he offers his hand, palm down as a Pope might offer his for obeisance.

A pleasure to make your acquaintance, sir.

HOLMES *and* **WATSON** *are astonished, then* **EDDY** *begins to tremble again, to drop to his knees and intone in Latin – a Catholic litany.*

He remains, hunched, silent, for a long moment, but then **HOLMES** *moves to touch his shoulder.*

HOLMES Sir...?

EDDY *turns a fear stricken face to him and:*

EDDY Save Annie. You must save Annie. I beg you – find her, protect her...hide her away.

HOLMES Save her from whom?

EDDY The Rippers stalk the streets. You must find her before it's too late...

WATSON *(overrides)* The Ripper? How does this concern the Ripper?

EDDY Even now he is looking for her.

HOLMES For Annie? Annie who? Who? Where shall I look for her?

EDDY Kelly knows. Mary Kelly. They think they've silenced her, but they haven't. She knows...she knows everything. She was there – with Annie and me. Annie...dearest Annie...

Suddenly he starts to tremble again.

You must help her. Help Annie.

His trembling now rapidly escalates into a kind of epileptic fit. **HOLMES** *and* **WATSON** *are hard pressed to hold him down, either on the floor or in a chair.*

WATSON Got to get something between his teeth. *Hold him!*

HOLMES *does, while* **WATSON** *finds a handkerchief, or perhaps even one of* **HOLMES**' *pipes, and forces it between* **EDDY**'*s teeth.*

HOLMES Epilepsy?

WATSON Hardly the time for a diagnosis, Holmes! Certainly a fit of some kind. There, old fellow, there...there...

Under **WATSON**'*s ministering hands and gentle tone,* **EDDY** *subsides into limp, semi-consciousness...*

Phew!

HOLMES What now?

WATSON *quickly checks* **EDDY**'*s pulse, lifts an eyelid, etc...*

WATSON Pulse rate's a bit high...but steady. Pupils dilated, on some kind of drug, probably something to calm him down... he'll be all right. Let him rest where he is. He'll come round in a while and probably remember nothing – not that he was remembering much before! Who is he, Holmes?

HOLMES I've no idea.

WATSON Yet you were expecting him.

HOLMES No. I was told to expect him. There is a difference.

They step back to regard **EDDY**.

I touched not a drop at dinner tonight.

WATSON *looks at him blankly –* **HOLMES** *proffers his glass.*

So another is in order.

WATSON Amen to that!

He moves to pour them both a stiff brandy, glancing back at **EDDY** *as:*

Poor devil, whoever he is.

HOLMES I agree with you, Watson. Although we know nothing of him, it is clear that he *has* "been hurt, and badly done by".

WATSON Wonder who this "Annie" woman is? Wife? Sister? (**HOLMES** *shrugs*) That's if she exists. And that business about the Ripper, did you put any credence to that?

HOLMES It was all most curious.

WATSON Mad. And that's what he is, I'm afraid. Poor fellow's obviously deranged, and what with the papers full of this dreadful Ripper business, sparing us damned few of the gory details...yes, chap unbalanced like this, would easily be affected by it.

HOLMES There is another possibility.

WATSON Oh?

HOLMES That he *is* the Ripper.

WATSON What?!

HOLMES *is conducting a quick, but keen, examination of the comatose* **EDDY**.

HOLMES The bandaging looks very professional to me.

WATSON Oh, yes, it's an expert job all right. *(Then he gets a sudden inspiration)* He's absconded from some hospital! Read too much about the Ripper – then you – one of the world's greatest criminologists...

HOLMES "One of"?

WATSON Well, you know what I mean, Holmes. Quite natural he should steer a path to your door. How's that? *(Beams)* Mystery solved, eh? Beat you at your own game! *(Frowns)* Except that somehow you knew he was coming. Can't see that one at all.

HOLMES *(smiles)* I'm withholding vital information from you, Watson.

WATSON Ah! Well, a chap can't be expected to make a *full* deduction if he's being cheated out of the whole picture.

HOLMES He recently wore a ring here. A heavy ring.

WATSON First thing they'd do in a hospital – remove all valuables.

HOLMES His jacket...

WATSON *(interjects)* Seen better days.

HOLMES Excellent, Watson. A totally accurate statement.

WATSON *(baffled)* It was?!

HOLMES "Grieves of Saville Row...tailors by appointment". I'd say our mystery man has seen better days too.

WATSON Unless he stole it.

HOLMES I doubt it. I would not expect the hands of a common thief to be this smooth. These have never done a day's work. The hairs of the beard on his cheek are fractionally shorter than those on his upper lip. Conclusion? Beat me at my own game on that one, Watson?

WATSON Ah...well...er...er...

HOLMES The conclusion is that the beard is newly acquired, but he has sported a moustache for some time.

WATSON Obviously! What will we do when he comes round? Shouldn't we contact some authority and...

HOLMES *(interjects)* No. We wait.

WATSON Wait for what?

HOLMES Someone to come for him.

At this moment the door bell jangles offstage. WATSON *is astonished.*

WATSON Good gracious, Holmes, this isn't some puppet play, is it? With you pulling the strings?

HOLMES Forewarned is forearmed.

As he speaks, he takes a revolver from desk and slips it into his pocket or waistband.

WATSON Another riddle!

MRS HUDSON *(offstage)* Here, wait a minute, where do you think you're going? Come back here...!

NETLEY *(offstage)* Out of my way.

Door bursts open and NETLEY *and another tough looking man named* POTTER *enter, hotly followed by* MRS HUDSON.

NETLEY *regards the unconscious* EDDY.

There he is.

MRS HUDSON I'm sorry, sir, soon as I opened the door, they pushed their way in and...

HOLMES *(interjects)* Thank you, Mrs Hudson, there is no need for concern.

As he speaks, he produces his revolver. This alarms MRS HUDSON *even more.*

MRS HUDSON Shall I send for the police, sir?

HOLMES *(cocking the gun)* That will not be necessary. *(She hesitates)* Leave us, please.

MRS HUDSON *(still reluctant)* Yes, sir. *(Then)* But I'll be just along the hall, sir... I'll hear if you call.

MRS HUDSON *exits.*

A tense moment as **HOLMES** *regards* **NETLEY** *and* **POTTER**.

NETLEY There's no need for that, sir.

HOLMES Is there not?

NETLEY We owe you an apology, Mr Holmes...

WATSON I should damned well think you do! Bursting in here, without a by your leave...

NETLEY We had to, gentlemen, thought you might be in danger. *(He regards* **EDDY***)* Been looking all over for him, we have. Followed him to Baker Street, then lost him...up and down we've been...then, I remembered him mentioning your name, sir. Oh, he looks harmless enough now, and probably been telling you all manner of fancy, fairy tales, I'll wager. But he can be very dangerous.

HOLMES We've seen no evidence of that.

NETLEY But that's the way they are, sir...crafty. *(To* **WATSON***)* You'd be Doctor Watson I imagine. *You'd* know.

HOLMES Who are you?

NETLEY Me, sir. I'm John Netley, and this here is Potter.

HOLMES *What* are you?

NETLEY Why we're...sort of male nurses, sir.

WATSON Nurses?!

NETLEY Not qualified, no, sir, and perhaps leaning more towards being a sort of guardian. Or caretaker! Yes, that's it, very caring we are. Taking care...of things, sir, and poor unfortunate people like him...difficult people. Dangerous people.

HOLMES For whom?

NETLEY The St. Giles Hospice, sir.

HOLMES *looks at* **WATSON**, *who nods:*

WATSON Yes, I've heard of it. South of the river – Blackfriars.

NETLEY That's the place, sir. Well, happily that's all sorted out, and again, gentlemen, my most humble apologies for the intrusion, but you can understand I'm sure, desperate situations call for desperate measures. Yes.

Moves towards **EDDY**.

Well, we'll be taking him off your hands now...

HOLMES Not just yet.

NETLEY *regards him.*

He is in your charge?

NETLEY Yes, sir.

HOLMES Then you'll know his name.

NETLEY Didn't he tell you that, sir...?

WATSON *(blurts out)* All he told us was a lot of nonsense about...

HOLMES *(quickly interjects)* He told us nothing of, credibility – and certainly not his name.

NETLEY Well, there's a problem there, sir...you see, a case like this...confidential, medical ethics, not the proper thing to do...

HOLMES I insist upon it. Or he remains here.

NETLEY Then again, you being *the* Sherlock Holmes and all, I don't see it can do any harm. He really didn't tell you, eh?

HOLMES No.

NETLEY Not doubting your word, sir, far from it. It's just so unusual, you see, he always gives some name. Likes names he does, all sorts of different names – why he's been General Gordon, the Prime Minister, a Prince of the Realm. Even thought he was Jack the Ripper on one occasion.

WATSON *reacts, looks at* **HOLMES**.

Funnily enough, just the other night, he thought he was *you*, Mr Holmes.

WATSON Good Lord!

HOLMES I have no wish to know who he *thinks* he is, but *who* he is!

NETLEY You wouldn't have ever heard of him, sir.

HOLMES Try me!

NETLEY His name's Devane, sir. Yes, that's right, Charles Devane. From a good family, but with a history of... *(Taps his head)* ...up here. It was the kindest thing – to put him in our caring hands.

HOLMES Devane?

NETLEY Yes, sir.

HOLMES Now you intend to return him to the Hospice.

NETLEY Those are our orders, sir.

HOLMES Naturally you would not be sent on such an errand without some form of written authority with Devane's name on it?

A moment; it seems as though **HOLMES** *has "got"* **NETLEY**, *but then he reaches into his pocket and produces a document.*

NETLEY Naturally.

He hands it to a frankly crestfallen **HOLMES**.

I always believe in being prepared, sir.

HOLMES *scans the document, then hands it to* **WATSON**, *who scans it, and:*

WATSON Perfectly in order.

NETLEY That's it then. *Potter.*

They bend to grip **EDDY**, *but again* **HOLMES** *intervenes.*

HOLMES Why is he bandaged?

NETLEY He had an operation, sir.

HOLMES What kind of operation?

NETLEY I think they call it a lobo, a lobot...something...

WATSON A lobotomy?

NETLEY That's it, sir.

Again **NETLEY** *and* **POTTER** *grip* **EDDY**, *and now start to lift him from the chair, prior to carrying/dragging him to the door. During this,* **EDDY** *stirs, his eyes open, he looks around – confused, then frightened.*

Again, my apologies for disturbing you, gentlemen...

EDDY No!

NETLEY Come along then, there's a good gentleman...

EDDY Don't let them take me...!

NETLEY Come on.

HOLMES *(overrides)* I'm sorry... I have no alternative.

EDDY Please!

And suddenly he breaks free and runs to grab **HOLMES** *– and stare into his face.*

You'll help? Promise me you'll help?

NETLEY's *voice has an edge to it now as he and* POTTER *grab* EDDY *again.*

NETLEY Now, you're not going to give us any trouble, are you...? That's it...

They drag EDDY *to the door – and at the last:*

EDDY *Promise me...!*

HOLMES Yes.

NETLEY *and* POTTER *exit with* EDDY. *Door closes and* HOLMES *remains, staring at it as:*

WATSON Lord, what an evening! Beginning to see how that chap Carroll came to write *Alice in Wonderland*!

HOLMES When a surgeon performs a lobotomy, he removes part of the brain, does he not?

WATSON Yes. No wonder the poor chap was as addled as a four-week egg!

HOLMES I shouldn't have let them take him.

WATSON Nothing else you could do. Even you can't flout the proper authority.

HOLMES Nevertheless...

Finally he turns from the door and:

But you are right, Watson, it was inevitable; "they will come to take him away". It had to be.

WATSON *(points a finger)* Holmes, there is a great deal you are not telling me.

HOLMES I admit it.

WATSON Eh?

HOLMES I don't want you to think me a fool, Watson.

WATSON What?! Oh, come now, Holmes, you surely know there is never any psosibility that I shall...

HOLMES There is a great deal I do not know myself. *(Then softly, angrily:)* But I mean to. *(Then, a change of manner:)* What did you make of the man Netley?

WATSON Nasty piece of work. I wouldn't trust him... *(Then, quickly:)* But that's just instinctive.

HOLMES I have come to value your instincts, Watson. A primeval barometer...no...! The needle of a compass...inexorably pointing to...the right path. And I share your instincts... yes, Netley *was* a "nasty piece of work". Also the seat of his trousers was shiny.

WATSON His trousers?

HOLMES Inordinately shiny. Would you not expect a nurse – guardian – caretaker – whatever he called himself – to spend more time on his feet than upon his backside? Not the case as far as Mr Netley is concerned. Shiny trousers, clear evidence that, whatever he does most, he does it sitting down.

WATSON *is baffled.*

WATSON Holmes, I don't care, I intend having another brandy! *(Then)* There's no way Mrs Hudson can find out, is there?

HOLMES I would rather you didn't, Watson.

WATSON Oh?

HOLMES I have work for you to do, and it will require a clear head.

WATSON *reacts, replaces stopper in decanter.*

WATSON Work? What kind of work?

HOLMES There was a Ripper murder tonight; according to the news seller, there were two.

WATSON The Ripper? Why concern ourselves with the Ripper?

HOLMES His name has woven through tonight's mystery.

WATSON I thought we'd discounted all that. Anyway, what mystery...? It was all solved.

HOLMES Not to my satisfaction. What's the name of that police surgeon you know so well?

WATSON Saunders.

HOLMES Go and seek him out, Watson, and lean heavily upon past favours.

WATSON To what end?

HOLMES *The Ripper!* Obtain access to the scene of the crime, then use that often so lucky nose of yours to sniff around. Glean what you can.

WATSON You are aware of the hour?

HOLMES While the trail is still fresh, my dear Watson.

WATSON *moves to the door, then hesitates, and:*

WATSON And what will *you* be doing?

HOLMES I intend seeking out our old friend Inspector Lestrade. There are many things I wish to ask him. Then...I want to find out more about Charles Devane.

Blackout.

Then, almost immediately, the downstage street lamp is illuminated again and **GULL** *and* **ANDERSON** *enter downstage to stroll up to the lamp and stop. Then, as their scene progresses, so we continue to bring up light downstage, signifying the approach of dawn and daylight.*

GULL *holds a scrap of paper – stopping now to examine it closely.*

GULL *(reads)* "The jews are the men that will not be blamed for nothing".

ANDERSON Note the spelling of the word "jews".

GULL "J.U.W.E.S." "ju-wes" – and this message was chalked up on a wall, you say?

ANDERSON At the scene of the crime, plain as a pikestaff for all to see.

GULL Thank heaven you acted so promptly. But how did you persuade the Commissioner to erase the words?

ANDERSON I reminded him it was his fraternal duty.

GULL again looks at the scrap of paper.

GULL "The jews"...? *(He proceeds to tear up the paper)* If that had got out – the way things are at the moment – there would have been more riots. Jewish shops looted – Jews attacked...there might have been a bloodbath tonight.

ANDERSON There was, Sir William. There was.

GULL and ANDERSON exit. LAMPLIGHTER enters to turn off the gas lamp and exit.

We illuminate an area of mean streets – part of a courtyard or narrow alleyway – where there is blood splashed on a wall – and SAUNDERS and WATSON survey the area.

SAUNDERS This is where they found the poor, wretched creature. To my mind, the worst to date. Her face was hideously mutilated, her nose cut off, lips, cheeks, forehead slashed open and flayed back, one ear almost severed and in addition...

WATSON In addition?!

SAUNDERS *(nods) In addition*, the throat was cut, the chest and abdomen cut open and the heart, lungs and intestines removed. If you wish, we can go back to the station – the official photographs should be ready by now, and you can see for yourself...

WATSON Just imagining it will be sufficient! Are you sure it happened here? I would have expected more blood.

SAUNDERS Ah, your friendship with Holmes rubs off. Yes, I too would have expected more blood. In fact I am convinced that the crime was committed elsewhere, and the remains dumped here after the poor woman was dead, but Anderson thinks otherwise.

WATSON Anderson?

SAUNDERS The new Assistant Commissioner. Insists the crime must have happened here. Mind you, I think he might be trying to protect the reputation of his street patrols...who were off chasing the first murder.

WATSON There were two then?

SAUNDERS Yes, first took place less than half a mile from here, a simple throat slitting. He must have been disturbed...but this one... He had her all to himself for as long as he needed.

WATSON Which again suggests it happened elsewhere – inside perhaps, out of sight?

SAUNDERS Yes. The mutilations must have taken some time.

WATSON Who was she?

SAUNDERS *(shrugs)* A street walker.

WATSON *(hard)* No, Saunders, *a human being*, and she had a name, didn't she?

SAUNDERS Eddowes. Catherine Eddowes. Mind you there's some confusion there. She'd been living with a man named Kelly these past few months, and taken to calling herself Mary Kelly.

WATSON Mary Kelly?!

Blackout this area and illuminate **HOLMES**' *chambers.* **HOLMES** *now wears the more familiar clothes we have come to associate with him, and stands, reading from a paper that he holds between another folded*

ACT I 33

paper – **MRS HUDSON** *bustles in to clear away some breakfast things.*

HOLMES "Sir, I send you half the kidney I took from one woman, prasarved it for you, t'other piece I fried and ate, it was very nise..."

MRS HUDSON What's that sir. Kidneys? Would you like kidneys for supper?

HOLMES Mrs Hudson, I doubt I may ever touch a kidney again.

MRS HUDSON *(puzzled)* Yes, sir.

Moves to exit – then pauses:

Kidneys are good for you. Better than drink!

Her point made, **MRS HUDSON** *exits with tray.*

HOLMES "I may send you the bloody knif...knife that took it out, if only you wate a whil...while longer. Catch me if you can..."

WATSON *enters from another room, towelling his hands dry.*

WATSON Glad to get the stench of that place off my hands. What have you got there?

HOLMES A letter from Jack the Ripper.

WATSON *reacts –* **HOLMES** *hands it to him, then withdraws it.*

Don't touch it. Keep it within the paper.

WATSON *takes it and reads it:*

WATSON Good Lord! *(Then)* A "knif", what's a "knif"?

HOLMES A misspelled knife.

WATSON They've had several of these things, haven't they?

HOLMES One was written in the blood of the victim.

WATSON What's the world coming to?!

He hands it back and **HOLMES** *studies it again.*

HOLMES You picked the most salient word.

WATSON I did?!

HOLMES Knife spelled K.N.I.F. – clear evidence that the writer is an educated man.

WATSON I wouldn't call that much of an education.

HOLMES But don't you see, my dear Watson, an illiterate man would have written N.I.F.E., not used the silent "K". The same is true of while…W.H.I.L…a man without benefit of schooling would be far more likely to write it W.I.L.E. No, this was written by a man at pains to conceal his education. And that's not all this letter tells us.

WATSON No?

HOLMES The fact that it, and the others, were written at all. Why suddenly try to mislead?

WATSON *stares at him.*

Because, somehow, the authorities were getting too close… At first they labelled the Ripper a maniac, a product of the streets he haunts – but then they began to conjecture that he might be a cleric, or a gentleman…

WATSON Some say he might be a doctor…or a policeman even.

HOLMES Exactly, and somewhere along the way, they touched upon a nerve – so he rushed into correspondence to put the lie to it, to affirm that he was – is – a rough and ignorant man. But I think he is not.

WATSON Well, I've told you how I got on, what about you – any luck?

HOLMES I spent several illuminating hours with Lestrade – he made me privy to this and other facts that have been kept concealed.

WATSON What about Charles Devane? Seems he was right about one thing – Mary Kelly.

HOLMES I later went to the St. Giles Hospice in Blackfriars.

WATSON And...?

HOLMES I didn't get past the front door. But I did learn that Charles Devane has been discharged and restored to the bosom of his family.

WATSON Eh? When?!

HOLMES In the early hours of this morning.

WATSON An unlikely story.

HOLMES Very unlikely.

WATSON Where have they taken him? Where's his family live?

HOLMES That, of course, was information they were unable to divulge.

WATSON I don't believe a word of it. Poor chap's been shanghaied, spirited away, but for what reason?

HOLMES Watson, we have stumbled onto something here – I'm not sure just what – but I am convinced it involves the Ripper murders, and Devane, and perhaps more than we could ever imagine.

He paces away for a moment, then:

Summarise the Ripper murders in a sentence.

WATSON The...er...the arbitrary murder of prostitutes in the East End of London.

HOLMES Splendid. But why the East End?

WATSON Because...that's where the victims are.

HOLMES Nonsense. Whores ply their trade all over London, one cannot cross the Haymarket without being accosted. And why does he continue in the East End – when the populace there is alerted, and police patrols trebled? Why does he not merely move to another, safer area...? Because the East End is where his targets are.

WATSON Targets?

HOLMES You said "arbitrary murders", and that's how they seem, but suppose they are not? Suppose they are part of an overall pattern?

WATSON Then there would have to be a common link between the victims?

HOLMES Exactly.

WATSON But it has been positively proved there isn't one.

HOLMES Of course there is, staring us in the face! Take horse racing!

WATSON What?!

HOLMES It occupies some thousands of people, takes place up and down the length of the country, but it is a closed world, Watson, and I'd wager there are few jockeys or trainers who have not encountered the other sometime! Yet here we are talking about perhaps less than a thousand prostitutes, walking the streets of an area that covers at most a square mile. Who is to say that one never met the other – *did not know the other*? The camaraderie of despair! Well?

WATSON Be damned difficult to prove.

HOLMES I'm talking possibility at the moment.

WATSON Very well, suppose you are right – where's it all leading?

HOLMES I don't know yet, Watson, but the prospect excites me.

During **HOLMES**' *big speech we have faintly heard the door bell jangle offstage.*

Now there is a tap at the door – then **MRS HUDSON** *enters and:*

MRS HUDSON A Mrs Mead to see you, sir.

KATE *enters.* HOLMES *regards her in a less sceptical manner than their first meeting.*

I told her you were busy, sir, but she said you would want to see her.

HOLMES Another accurate prediction. My dear Mrs Mead, how pleasant to see you again.

As he speaks, he takes her hands and draws her into the room. His frankly admiring attitude does not go un-noticed by WATSON *or* MRS HUDSON, *both of whom are very intrigued.*

May I introduce my good friend and colleague, Doctor Watson? Mrs Katherine Mead.

KATE Doctor Watson.

WATSON How do you do?

HOLMES Will you take some tea with us?

KATE Thank you, no.

HOLMES Then that will be all, Mrs Hudson.

MRS HUDSON *(very reluctant to go)* Yes, sir. *(Then)* Should you need anything else, sir, I'll be nearby.

HOLMES I'm sure you will.

MRS HUDSON *exits.*

Please.

This to KATE *as he sits her down and takes chair opposite her.*

Now. You know of course that your mysterious man turned up here last night? Yes, I can see it in your eyes that you know.

KATE Who he is? Did you discover that?

HOLMES I was told – Charles Devane. Do you think that is correct?

KATE *(thinks)* No.

HOLMES Nor I. But the murders you spoke of, I think they are the Ripper murders.

KATE That's why I am here, Mr Holmes. Since I spoke to you my mind has been in turmoil. I have "seen" so many things, ghastly, cruel things, but it is all mixed up, nothing is clear. But this morning I was shopping in Bond Street, then suddenly I felt compelled to turn into Grafton Street; I had no reason to go there, it is all book shops and art galleries, but something drew me there, and I found myself staring into the window of a gallery where there is an exhibition of paintings by Walter Sickert...

There is a pause as she trails off, lost in her thoughts and memory of the moment.

HOLMES And...?

KATE I began to weep. I felt such an overwhelming sense of sadness... But there was one picture...

Again, she cannot continue.

HOLMES What of it?

KATE It's something I think you should see for yourself, Mr Holmes.

He regards her a moment, then:

HOLMES Very well. Watson, would you be so kind as to go and summon a hansom for myself and Mrs Mead?

To her:

We will go there immediately.

WATSON *nods and, pretty baffled by the whole thing, moves to exit.*

It is a remarkable gift that you have, Mrs Mead.

KATE No, not a gift, a curse! To suffer the pain of others...?!

HOLMES Yes. Nevertheless...

> **HOLMES** *gets to his feet to go and get something from a box on his desk.*

...would you grant me a favour?

KATE If I can.

HOLMES You recall, when you took my hand that first time, you spoke of a lady with red hair...and a brooch made of entwined serpents? *(He extends brooch to her)* This brooch.

> **KATE** *takes it, regards it.*

It was returned to me a year ago. By hand, so there was no postmark. Nor was there a note.

> **KATE** *regards the brooch and then* **HOLMES** *speaks with a passion we have never seen before:*

Where is she? What has become of her? Find her for me!

> **KATE** *holds the brooch, turning it over and over, then holding it tight against her bosom, "concentrating" on it for a few moments, then:*

KATE Must you know?

HOLMES Yes.

KATE She is dead.

> **HOLMES** *reacts, moves to lean on desk with both hands, the attitude of his body expressing his anguish. Finally:*

HOLMES There can be no doubt?

KATE No. I'm sorry.

HOLMES She was so vital... How did she die?

KATE Mr Holmes...

HOLMES *(overrides) Tell me how*!

    KATE *again holds and "concentrates" on brooch:*

    Now – and this is optional – but could make for wonderful theatre and also be reprised later when we find Annie: As **KATE** *"concentrates" we slowly build up the Sound Effects of Bedlam – literally, the screams and sounds of the inmates of an asylum, beginning softly, rising up, up to an almost unbearable crescendo, and then, as* **KATE** *"finds out" – abruptly cut as:*

KATE *(reluctant to impart what she has "seen")* Isn't it enough to know she is dead? Must you punish yourself further...?

HOLMES *(overrides) How*?!

KATE In an asylum for the insane.

    HOLMES *reacts: During this sequence he has completely and untypically lost his control and composure – and with it, we see behind the veil, we have humanised him.*

    For some moments he does not trust himself to speak, but then, finally, he moves to take the brooch back from **KATE**, *place it back in the box and:*

HOLMES *(calm again)* I am obliged to you.

    WATSON *enters.*

WATSON Got the cab waiting.

HOLMES Thank you, Watson.

    As he prepares to leave with **KATE** – **WATSON** *regards him, hoping to be invited.*

WATSON I could squeeze in too, if you want me?

HOLMES No, thank you, Watson.

    HOLMES *and* **KATE** *move to exit.*

WATSON You might need a second opinion!

But they exit. **WATSON** *paces grumpily away.*

One of these days I will write those memoirs, then you'll see – I'll have equal importance!

Blackout – and immediately we illuminate the art gallery. This could be just a few paintings suspended – flown in – or a few on easels. We do not have to see the paintings, they can be angled upstage. **BRADBURY** *is in the act of taking one down.*

HOLMES *and* **KATE** *enter.*

BRADBURY Sorry, gallery's closed, exhibition officially finished yesterday.

HOLMES We might be potential buyers.

BRADBURY Nice. Wouldn't do you any good though. Everything's sold. That's what I'm doing, getting 'em ready for collection.

KATE *steers* **HOLMES** *to look at a particular painting.*

HOLMES Even this one?

BRADBURY No, that one never was for sale. Express instructions of Sickert, "Display prominently, but do not sell".

HOLMES And where is Sickert now?

BRADBURY Run off to Dieppe.

HOLMES Run off?

BRADBURY Looked that way to me. "Indecent haste" at the very least. Saw the pictures hung – then off to Dieppe on the first steamer.

KATE It's a most unusual subject.

BRADBURY Yes, who'd think of painting a girl lying murdered on her bed? I shouldn't have thought anyone would have wanted to buy it anyway. (*At* **KATE**) Or a decent young lady should be looking at it!

HOLMES "The Camden Town Murders".

BRADBURY I think that was an afterthought. The original title was... (*He looks at back of painting*) ...yes... "The jews are not the men..." can't read the rest of it. Can't even spell "jews" either! No title at all is it? He did another like this... I didn't even bother to hang it...

HOLMES Do you have it here? May we see?

BRADBURY Why not?

> **BRADBURY** *exits.* **HOLMES** *and* **KATE** *regard the painting.*

HOLMES "Juwes". Inspector Lestrade told me a similar inscription was found near to the last Ripper murder.

> *He becomes aware that* **KATE** *is rigid, staring at the painting. Then, very reluctantly, she reaches out her hand to touch it.*

What is it? What do you feel?

KATE Anguish. Guilt... As though Sickert were trying to warn us.

> *She gasps, steps rapidly away from the painting.*

I don't know, I don't know.

> **BRADBURY** *enters, carrying a painting.*

BRADBURY There we are, now look at this: another girl on her bed...but look at her face. *That's* no way to paint a face, is it? Looks as though her nose has been cut off, looks... mutilated...dreadful I call it.

HOLMES Do you know the artist well?

BRADBURY Been Sickert's agent on and off for years now, made a shilling or two between us, we have. Yes, pretty well.

HOLMES Then you must know Charles Devane?

BRADBURY Devane? No, I don't recall...

HOLMES Annie then?

BRADBURY Annie? Oh, you must mean Annie Crooks! Yes, she posed for him a couple of times, I think, back in the old days at Cleveland Street... Yes... Annie...pretty little thing.

HOLMES Where is she now?

BRADBURY Annie? Oh, I dunno, lost touch, she got married, moved on...

HOLMES Where was she married?

BRADBURY Not sure. Somewhere in London.

HOLMES It'll be a matter of record then. Thank you.

HOLMES and KATE move to exit. BRADBURY gazes after them, then at the picture he still holds.

BRADBURY Dreadful. No way to treat a lady.

Blackout and immediately illuminate:

HOLMES' chambers. Empty for a beat, and then MRS. HUDSON enters with a tea tray – puts it down, looks around, and at this moment KATE enters through door to other areas of chambers.

MRS HUDSON I expect you found it a bit spartan, Madam?

KATE regards her.

Mr Holmes' bathroom. I've said so many times, let me put a bit of chintz at the window, or some nice pink soap – some of that Sunlight with the little girl on the poster...he won't have it. Mind you, there was a time...anyway, I've put out the best china as you can see – may not be chintz or pink, but it *is* ladylike. Delicate.

KATE Thank you, Mrs Hudson.

MRS HUDSON It *is Mrs* Mead, isn't it, Madam?

KATE *(regards her)* I am a widow, Mrs Hudson.

MRS HUDSON *(pleased)* Oh. This china hasn't been used in a long while.

KATE Since the lady with the red hair.

MRS HUDSON Oh! He's told you about her, has he?

KATE In a manner, yes.

MRS HUDSON You are privileged then. He hasn't spoke of her in such a long while. They were happy times – the best china was used every day. You know, madam, apart from the fact that your hair isn't red, you are very like her.

KATE *Am I?!*

MRS HUDSON He didn't tell you that? *(Rather satisfied by this conclusion:)* Well, he hasn't told you everything then.

HOLMES *enters.*

Just served tea, sir.

HOLMES *(vaguely)* Good. Excellent.

MRS HUDSON In the best china, sir.

MRS HUDSON *exits.*

HOLMES I inquired at the ticket office. A clerk there recalls Sickert quite clearly, not just because of his wild manner, but because under his arm he carried a teddy bear.

KATE A teddy bear!

HOLMES He reserved a cabin, and his ticket was one way.

KATE Then he *is* running away.

HOLMES With no immediate intention of returning. I telegraphed Dieppe. Our painter keeps a studio there, but he has gone, moved on. Still running, it seems, but why?

KATE In fear.

HOLMES But of what?

KATE *(shrugs, sighs)* This whole confused business...

HOLMES Mrs Mead...

KATE *(interjects)* Please, I would prefer "Kate".

HOLMES *(hesitates)* Kate, then. Now then...

KATE *(interjects)* Does anyone ever call you "Sherlock".

HOLMES *(a bit taken aback)* Very few. Would it please you to?

> *She regards him.*
>
> If so, it would please me.

KATE Suppose I'm wrong? These...visions... I have been wrong before you know.

HOLMES Not this time.

KATE I would like to be wrong. Then that would be an end to it, wouldn't it?

HOLMES No. And if you were...at least I met you.

KATE Am I very like her?

> **HOLMES** *is taken off balance by the question. Then, realising:*

HOLMES Mrs Hudson!

KATE She meant no harm. *(She smiles a rare smile)* She would like everything to be pink and chintz.

> **HOLMES** *takes her hands.*

HOLMES Kate...

> **WATSON** *enters and* **HOLMES** *instantly lets go* **KATE***'s hands and steps back.* **WATSON** *is puffed and excited and waves a paper:*

WATSON Holmes, I've got it...took hours of burrowing through the files but I've got it. *(In triumph)* Copy of a certificate of a marriage between a William Gorman *and one Annie Crooks!*

HOLMES *snatches it from him, scans it and:*

HOLMES "17th of March 1884, in the parish of St. Marylebone... William Gorman and Ann Crooks of..."

WATSON *(interjects)* Look at the witnesses!

HOLMES Walter Sickert and... *Mary Kelly!*

WATSON There, what about that then? Oh, good day, Mrs Mead... *(To* HOLMES*)* Didn't I do well?!

HOLMES Superlatively, my dear Watson. At last a definite, link...! But to what?

WATSON Eh? *(Deflation setting in)* I did what you told me to.

HOLMES Of course you did, and you have my congratulations – but where next? Kate?

KATE I'm sorry.

She gestures, and then sways and clutches chair for support. HOLMES *quickly moves to her.*

HOLMES What is it, are you unwell?

KATE It has been a long day. I'm tired.

HOLMES You must be. And I the insensitive fool who did not notice.

WATSON But, Holmes, you notice everything.

HOLMES Let me take you home.

KATE That won't be necessary, but if you could put me into a cab...

HOLMES Right away. *(Supporting her)* Come...

As they move to exit:

KATE Thank you, Sherlock.

They exit and **WATSON** *turns to stare after them, thunderstruck by the "Sherlock". Then he moves away and starts to pour himself a drink.*

WATSON Well...fine thanks for a weary day at Somerset House – "Where next"?! Enough that I found the damned certificate – it's quite obvious there is a clear link to... *(Falters)* A clear link to... *(Then, arrogantly proffers glass)* Dammit, Mrs Hudson, don't care if you *do* see me drinking at this time of day!

He drinks – and at this moment the door opens and **WATSON**, *thinking it might be* **HUDSON**, *gags on the drink, thrusts the glass behind his back.* **HOLMES** *enters.* **WATSON** *watches him as he moves to the window to gaze off – then wave to* **KATE** *– offstage – as she departs.*

She called you "Sherlock".

HOLMES *regards him absently.*

I never call you Sherlock.

HOLMES As you well know, Watson, it is a name foisted upon me by well meaning, but misguided parents. A name I abhor.

WATSON Didn't seem to mind much when she said it.

HOLMES *She* is a lady.

WATSON Brilliant piece of deduction!

HOLMES Petulance does not sit well on you, Watson.

WATSON Petulant? Who's petulant?

HOLMES *moves to put his arm around* **WATSON**'s *shoulders.*

HOLMES My dear old friend, you have done a splendid job.

WATSON You think so?

HOLMES I do, and I'm very, very grateful to you.

WATSON Oh, don't mention it. I'm not after praise you know.

HOLMES *moves to pick up the copy certificate again and study it.*

HOLMES There is something not right.

WATSON It's an exact copy.

HOLMES I'm not doubting that. "17th of March, 1884." *(paces away, then stops:)* Watson, the last Ripper murder, Catherine…?

WATSON *(interjects)* Eddowes.

HOLMES Eddowes. Also known as Mary Kelly…and didn't Saunders tell you *how* she came to be known by that name?

WATSON Yes, she'd been living with a man named Kelly these past few months and…

HOLMES *(interjects) These past few months*! Yet *our* Mary Kelly was witness at a wedding in 1884, *four years ago*! Don't you see, Watson…?

At this moment, the door bursts open and **KATE** *rushes in.*

KATE It suddenly came to me. The Ripper… If Mary Kelly was his intended victim…

HOLMES *(interjects)* …he killed the wrong woman! Which means the real Mary Kelly is still alive! And he'll try again if we don't stop him!

Blackout.

Now, during the blackout, we creep in the Sound Effects of an East End pub of the period; a babble of voices, glasses clinking, and people singing a song of the period to a jangling old piano. This sound is muted at this time.

We tightly illuminate an area up stage right – where a free standing pub door obliquely faces upstage. The name of pub or brewers is on the door, but, since we are seeing it from the inside, it is "mirror" writing.

NETLEY enters the light beyond the door – and as he does so, a DRUNK goes through the door from the pub to the outside where NETLEY is.

En route, the DRUNK almost collides with NETLEY, who grabs the DRUNK with powerful hands and demands:

NETLEY I'm looking for a woman named Kelly. Have you seen her?

DRUNK Mary? She's in the pub.

NETLEY brutally thrusts the DRUNK away and turns towards the pub door. Now he moves to enter the door, and, as he comes through to stand the other side, we hold him in spotlight, and at the same time, we bring up the Sound Effects of the pub very loud indeed.

NETLEY remains, looking across the dark expanse of stage – then suddenly we hear KELLY laugh and we spotlight her downstage left, either standing, or seated at a table, but with the door obliquely behind her, and her head thrown back in drunken laughter.

NETLEY regards her – then suddenly his intense stare "gets through" to MARY KELLY, who, sensing something, spins round and she and NETLEY stare at each other across the dark, intervening space. Then KELLY drops her glass and runs away to exit stage left. NETLEY quickly moves to pursue her.

Curtain falls on:

End of Act One

ACT II

Scene One

The curtain rises on:

A restricted downstage area is illuminated as: a section of London embankment. Just a fraction of wall purporting to be overlooking the river – perhaps adorned with one of the distinctive lamps of that area.

GULL leans on the wall, staring out – somewhere a ship's foghorn mournfully sounds.

ANDERSON enters.

ANDERSON Sir William?

GULL Anderson...you summoned me from an excellent dinner.

ANDERSON Good of you to come, but I thought it imperative we meet. You will read it in *The Times* tomorrow, but I can tell you now, Sir Charles Warren has resigned as Commissioner.

GULL For what reason?

ANDERSON I think his "fraternal duty" weighed too heavily upon him.

GULL He admitted that?!

ANDERSON The official statement will say that he has "pressing family commitments", while the papers will surmise it is because of the criticism of his handling of the recent riots – of his attitude to the unemployed.

ACT II, SCENE ONE

GULL Thank God for that!

ANDERSON Thank *me*, Sir William, I am nearer than God at this time. Sir Charles had developed a conscience. I had to be very persuasive.

GULL You don't think he will have second thoughts...?

ANDERSON I warned him that, should that occur, his brothers might sever all connections with him. *Sever*. I stressed the word carefully.

GULL Then I do thank you, Anderson. But God too – He knows what lengths we go to – to keep this country of ours clean and straight, and with our Monarch still at the helm. With Warren gone, where will you stand now?

ANDERSON I expect I shall have free rein for a while.

GULL You can step up the patrols, eh? Increased vigilance – this Kelly woman...

ANDERSON *(interjects)* ...is the last of the Ripper's intended victims.

GULL Which means she *must* be found...and then you, personally, can write an end to the murders. A feather in your cap.

ANDERSON Don't worry – she will be found. *(Then)* Well, then, what is it to be, Sir William...a return to your excellent dinner – or a drink at my club? It is just a short walk across the bridge there.

GULL A brisk walk, followed by a warming glass? Yes, I would enjoy that.

ANDERSON Very well, then...

As they turn to move away – **GULL** *pauses and shouts back into the darkness:*

GULL Driver – follow us across the bridge!

NETLEY *(offstage)* Yes, sir.

ANDERSON *and* GULL *move to exit, and now we hear the Sound Effects of a hansom starting to follow: rattle of harness, creak of wheels and carriage, the clop of horses' hooves.*

Lose lights on downstage "set" and now spotlight:

THE BLIND BEGGAR, *"dossed down", as we shall see, on the upper level of this complex. He wears milk white spectacles, carries a white stick and nearby is his tray of matches for sale. His hair is straggling out from under his cap, and his sideburns are ill kempt – he sports a scrubby beard. His clothes are a hodge podge, and quite filthy. He looks like a man in disguise. He sleeps fitfully.*

We establish him – and then (if possible using a follow spot to evoke a cinematic pan) we pan away to pick up and spotlight the PREACHER.

If follow spot is impracticable then we merely extinguish one, illuminate another.

The PREACHER *is on the lower level. He might be a Salvation Army man, but, to avoid giving offence to that organisation, and also – in preference – I see him as a paunchy man, clad in black, with long raw-boned hands and wrists that have outgrown the sleeves of his jacket, with a gleaming bald head, but with a mass of wild hair growing wildly around his pate. He sports a large, luxuriant beard, and his voice booms with a Welsh accent as:*

PREACHER Oh, hear me, brothers and sisters, hear me in the name of the Lord. Some say that the Devil himself stalks these dark streets, but I say it is Retribution. The wrath of God – who seeks out the evil doer – who smites down those who sin against his word...

STREET WALKER *enters the overspill of the spotlight and pauses a moment.*

ACT II, SCENE ONE

STREETWALKER Hello, dearie.

PREACHER Repent now, sister, I beg you to repent now.

STREETWALKER Oh, I would. Right away I would. Don't do it for love you know...do it to feed me mouth. What do you know about poverty? About Sin? Oh, I could tell you...

PREACHER You have something to impart to me?

STREETWALKER Impart?! Oh, yes, dearie, I've got to impart all right...

STREETWALKER takes one pace away, stops and regards him, then tosses her head coquettishly, wriggling her hips.

I could tell you a few things that would take your breath away – things that'd make your hair curl. What's left of it.

STREETWALKER *laughs and moves to exit.*

PREACHER *(soft)* Could you now?

PREACHER, *suddenly a menacing figure, moves to exit after the* **STREETWALKER.**

Now we fully illuminate (albeit that the scene remains dark and shadowy) the East End area.

There are two levels – perhaps suggesting the proximity of a wharf. A platform or street area stands about ten feet above the lower level, the two connected by stone steps. The lower level has a doorway/alley/archway whereby a person can stand, out of sight from those above, yet still be clearly heard.

Far off we can perhaps hear a barrel organ and other muted street sounds.

About halfway along the upper level the **BEGGAR** *sleeps.*

WATSON *enters on the upper level – looks along it and:*

WATSON "Third buttress from the end".

> *He starts to count them off (although for "buttresses" we could read "lanterns" or whatever, and amend dialogue accordingly).*

> One...two...three.

> *As he reaches "three", he finds himself almost hard up against* BEGGAR.

> Oh!

> *The* BEGGAR *flings out a hand to touch* WATSON.

BEGGAR Spare a copper, sir? Matches, sir? Buy the wares of a poor blind man?

> *He suddenly strikes a brightly flaring match.*

> Lucifers, sir. I'm told they burn with a high, bright flame!

> WATSON *almost gets his whiskers singed! He dodges to one side as:*

WATSON For God's sake man...you nearly singed my whiskers!

BEGGAR Oh, sorry, sir...sorry...

> *As* BEGGAR *speaks, he turns to extend the match the other way – and nearly gets* WATSON*'s whiskers again!*

> WATSON *extinguishes the match with an almighty puff.*

> You'll buy some then, sir...? To help a poor blind man...?

WATSON Yes, yes, I'll have a box of the damned things.

> *He slaps some money in* BEGGAR*'s hand – and takes a box of matches.*

BEGGAR Thank you kindly, sir.

> *He pockets the money and* WATSON *regards him.*

ACT II, SCENE ONE 55

WATSON Well then, off you go.

BEGGAR Go, sir?

WATSON You've made your sale – you can run along now.

BEGGAR Oh, I couldn't do that, sir.

WATSON Why not?!

BEGGAR This is my pitch sir. I always stand here.

WATSON That may be, but it just so happens that I have arranged to meet someone here – this exact spot – a very confidential meeting.

BEGGAR I see, sir.

Then – a wicked smile and nudge:

A lady is it, sir?

WATSON No, it is not a lady, and for that matter, none of your damned business. *(Controls himself:)* What if I were to purchase all you matches?

BEGGAR Every one?

WATSON Yes.

BEGGAR Oh, that would be nice, sir.

WATSON Good.

Slaps a note into **BEGGAR**'s *hand:*

Settled then.

BEGGAR *feels the note and then proffers the tray to* **WATSON**.

No, you can keep the matches.

BEGGAR Oh, that *is* good of you, sir...

WATSON Goodbye then.

BEGGAR Goodbye, sir.

Neither moves – a pause – then:

Are you leaving?

WATSON NO! *You* are!

BEGGAR Oh, I couldn't, sir.

WATSON WHY NOT?!

BEGGAR With all this money you give me? I wouldn't trust myself walking the streets alone. I'll have to wait until my niece arrives to lead me home.

WATSON Now, look here – do you know who you're dealing with?!

BEGGAR No, sir...

WATSON Well... Sherlock Holmes, that's who!

BEGGAR The famous detective?!

WATSON The very same.

BEGGAR My friends won't believe I've seen you, sir.

WATSON Well, you haven't, have you? In your condition!

Then, a sudden suspicion:

What the devil are you doing here, anyway?

BEGGAR Selling matches, sir.

WATSON To whom? Nobody's passed by since I arrived – and I should think nobody will. It's a dead end this place...

Suddenly grabs **BEGGAR**:

Holmes!

BEGGAR No, sir. *You're* Holmes!

WATSON You've played this little charade once too often, but I see through it this time...let's get those stupid whiskers off...

He grabs **BEGGAR**'s *whiskers, pulls, and the* **BEGGAR** *cries out, and the whiskers stay firm!*

ACT II, SCENE ONE

WATSON Good Lord.

At this moment we hear a woman scream offstage. **WATSON** *freezes for a moment, then, releasing the* **BEGGAR**, *and tugging out his pistol, he hurries to the edge of the upper level. As he does so –* **PREACHER** *enters on lower level.*

You! Stand firm! Put your hands in the air.

PREACHER *freezes as* **WATSON**, *fully in command, points the pistol.*

Then, in a triumphant aside to **BEGGAR**:

The Ripper. We've got him.

BEGGAR, *who wants no trouble, scrambles to his feet, grabbing up his cane, and starting to hurry away.*

BEGGAR Well, Sherlock Holmes always gets his man, doesn't he?

WATSON Holmes? *The name is Watson.* Come back here...you're an eye witness.

BEGGAR *hurries away to exit,* **WATSON** *momentarily diverted from* **PREACHER**.

Well, perhaps not an *eye* witness.

He firmly trains the pistol on **PREACHER** *again.*

Come up here. Stay in the light.

PREACHER *ascends to the upper level.*

Now then...

PREACHER You are a formidable figure, Watson. I feel safe with you.

WATSON Holmes?! You can't be. It's a trick... I heard a woman scream!

PREACHER/HOLMES I said to meet me at the third buttress *below* this level, and if you had spent as much time as I have today, wandering these mean streets, you would come to know that the scream of a woman, a child and, yes, even a man, is commonplace.

WATSON You *did* bring me here to have a good laugh at my expense.

HOLMES On the contrary, I brought you here for a most serious purpose. Shh!

This, as he pulls **WATSON** *into the shadows as, on the lower level, a* **POLICEMAN** *enters, prowls around, pausing to play his bulls-eye lamp around the dark area, and then move on to exit.*

A most serious purpose. To find Mary Kelly. In this guise I have been prowling these mean streets for some hours – watching – and spreading the word.

WATSON, *despite himself, picks up* **HOLMES'** *whisper:*

WATSON What word?

HOLMES That I seek only to help Mary Kelly, and twenty guineas awaits anyone who turns up at this spot with news of her whereabouts. That's why I wanted you here. Twenty guineas! In an area where men would murder for half that amount? I need you at my back, my good and faithful friend.

WATSON You can rely on me, Holmes.

HOLMES I know that well. But remain in the shadows there, Watson... Whoever, if ever someone comes, it will be reassuring if they see only an Evangelist.

WATSON *moves away to a shadowy area.* **HOLMES** *remains at a prominent position on the upper level.*

A moment, then, in whispers:

It's a cold night.

ACT II, SCENE ONE

WATSON Bitter.

HOLMES I wish I'd had the wit to ask you to bring along a flask.

WATSON You think I didn't?!

He starts to step out of the shadows, producing a hip flask when:

On the lower level **MARY KELLY** *enters, muffled in a shawl, a barely discernible figure, who immediately stops in the shadows, yet* **HOLMES** *detects the movement and urgently gestures to* **WATSON** *that he return into the shadows – while* **HOLMES** *waits.*

A moment, and then:

KELLY *(whispers)* Hey – you up there...

HOLMES *moves to gaze down.*

You been asking about a Mary Kelly...?

HOLMES Yes.

KELLY Who are you?

HOLMES A friend – who wants only to help.

KELLY You ain't no Preacher.

HOLMES I'm no murderer either – come up here, or let me come down to you...

KELLY *(presses back into shadows)* I ain't stupid.

HOLMES *produces purse, shakes it.*

HOLMES Twenty golden guineas, and yours if you can lead me to Mary Kelly.

KELLY What do you want with her?

HOLMES She is in great danger...

KELLY She knows that!

HOLMES *reacts – then points a finger.*

HOLMES You are Mary Kelly...

He moves.

KELLY Stay where you are or I'll run...

HOLMES Here. An act of good faith.

He tosses down the purse. **KELLY** *sneaks out of the shadows to snatch it up, then darts back again. Then, becoming a bit more reassured...*

KELLY It ain't just the money. You promised to help... I can't hide forever and...

At this moment **WATSON** *quickly stifles a cough, and* **KELLY**, *alarmed:*

There's someone else up there with you...

She starts to move away – but:

HOLMES No...don't go. I am Sherlock Holmes!

This causes her to pause uncertainly. **HOLMES** *peels off most of his disguise as:*

Sherlock Holmes. And yes, there *is* someone here with me...

He gestures and **WATSON** *moves forward.*

My good friend, Doctor Watson. Can we not talk face to face...?

He makes to start down the steps, but **KELLY**'*s fear returns – and she backs away –* **HOLMES** *stops dead immediately, fearful of scaring her away as:*

All right, all right, I'll come no nearer, I promise you. But you are in fearful danger.

KELLY *(hefts the purse)* Not now I've got this. Can get back to my sister in Dublin with this.

ACT II, SCENE ONE

HOLMES Not before you've told me about Annie Crooks.

KELLY How'd you know about Annie?!

HOLMES From a man named Charles Devane – you must know him?

KELLY Devane? Nah!

HOLMES But you are the Mary Kelly who was a witness at Annie's wedding?

KELLY Yes.

HOLMES Who *is* Annie Crooks?

KELLY Why – Annie...? She's just Annie, that's all.

HOLMES How did you meet?

KELLY Worked together we did – I was going straight then – worked at a tobacconists in Cleveland Street...

HOLMES Cleveland Street – is that how you came to know the artist, Sickert?

KELLY Walter? Yes, he was always in and out. Annie posed for him a couple of times. Oh, but all proper it was, I was there and she didn't take off a stitch!

HOLMES Sickert was a witness at the wedding.

KELLY Yes, witness to everything, then and since!

HOLMES What do you mean?

KELLY I've got to get going.

HOLMES Tell me about Annie's husband!

KELLY *(hesitates)* Eddy?

HOLMES Eddy? Her wedding certificate says he was "William Gorman".

KELLY Well...we called him Eddy – sort of nickname...

HOLMES What about him? Who is he?

KELLY He's the reason...

HOLMES What do you mean?

KELLY I ain't going to say any more about Eddy... I told the others about him, and look where they ended up – in the morgue!

HOLMES What did you tell them...?

KELLY About him and Annie, now that's enough!

She turns as though to go, but:

HOLMES No. Don't go! Not alone through these dark streets, and the Ripper still on the prowl.

She hesitates.

Where can I find Annie Crooks?

KELLY I don't know. They came and took her away...

HOLMES Who?

KELLY Men came for her... I don't know...

HOLMES Took her where?

KELLY I don't know that either. If I did, I'd tell you – Annie needs help, that I do know...poor soul...and she so good... and so *shining* as she stood there on her wedding day. A good Catholic girl, and so proud of her Eddy – because she never thought he'd stand by her... He did though, until *they* stepped in.

HOLMES The same men who took Annie away...?

KELLY I dunno. The same type.

HOLMES Was Sickert one of them?

KELLY He was part of it, yes...but he's made up since then... *atoned*... He kept Alice from them...took her and hid her... and now he's run off with her...

HOLMES Alice? Who is Alice?

ACT II, SCENE ONE

KELLY I said enough already. I said too much...

HOLMES moves to start slowly, but resolutely down towards her as:

HOLMES Let Watson and I escort you to my chambers – where you will be safe, and we can talk more until it is time for you to take the ship to Dublin...

During this we hear the Sound Effects of the approach of a hansom, and – if it is possible – it would be a bonus to terminate the scene by seeing the actual shadow of a hansom somewhere in the area.

HOLMES and WATSON are barely aware of it – but KELLY hears it right away, and is profoundly frightened by it and its implications. Suddenly she backs away from the sound.

What is wrong?

KELLY turns and runs off into the shadows to exit. HOLMES plunges after her.

No, wait...come back here...

To WATSON:

Watson, we must find her!

And as HOLMES and WATSON run off too – and we blackout, so the Sound Effects of hansom cab reaches crescendo – and then, ominously, it stops.

Then, KELLY is illuminated, on her knees, praying in a church. This is, in the main, created by Lighting Effects – a spotlight shining through a cut-out so that KELLY kneels in the light created by, and apparently shining through, a distinctive church window. If we can also juxtapose her to some religious icon too, that would be nice.

KELLY intones – in Latin – a Catholic litany, asking forgiveness and protection.

During this, **NETLEY** *enters and stalks up behind her.* **KELLY** *remains unaware until* **NETLEY** *seizes her by the throat from behind and drags her, making choking sounds, away to exit.*

Blackout – and immediately, dimly illuminate the East End area.

HOLMES *enters, moving slowly, turning this way and that, looking for* **KELLY** *– and then he reacts to the faint Sound Effects of a hansom cab – receding –* **HOLMES** *moves towards the receding sound and suddenly, hopefully, startlingly,* **WATSON** *steps out of a dark area and collides with* **HOLMES***!*

HOLMES *instantly steps back, his sword stick half drawn from its sheath – while* **WATSON** *pulls a pistol – and they stare at each other, then relax a bit as:*

WATSON Holmes, this is hopeless. Damned place is a labyrinth. Reminds me of the Casbah without the colour. Why on earth did she run off in the first place?

HOLMES Fear.

WATSON Of what? The sound of a hansom cab! Seems ridiculous to me.

HOLMES But to me – significant.

WATSON Holmes...

HOLMES Shhh!

They stand in silence as again we hear Sound Effects of a hansom cab suddenly whipped up and racing away, receding. **HOLMES** *turns towards the source of the sound and:*

ACT II, SCENE ONE

This way!

HOLMES and **WATSON** *hurry off to exit.*

Now, it would be desirable (and probably under cover of blackout?) to use trucks to subtly change the East End street and bring in a brick wall, with a small window set into it, but the remainder of the wall gauzed so as to become transparent when lit, and show a view into **KELLY**'s *bedsitting room. Alternatively, we stay with the existing set, but make provision for a window and "gauzed" brick wall within it.*

Illuminate this area and then **NETLEY** *and* **GULL** *enter, from an area upstage – purporting to have exited an unseen door that leads into* **KELLY**'s *bedsitter.*

There is an urgency about them, and **NETLEY** *is using his cape to deliberately muffle* **GULL**'s *face (to such effect that we should not be aware it is* **GULL** *at this juncture).* **GULL**'s *hands are red with blood – and* **NETLEY**'s *too.*

HOLMES *(offstage)* Watson...?

WATSON *(offstage)* Over here.

NETLEY *reacts to the voices and then, urging* **GULL** *away:*

NETLEY Get into the cab. Wait for me there.

GULL *exits and* **NETLEY** *takes up a position in the shadows to watch and wait as:*

HOLMES *and* **WATSON** *enter this, to all intents and purposes, "new" area of the East End.*

They stop and listen.

WATSON A labyrinth. A damned labyrinth!

HOLMES Shh!

WATSON I hear nothing.

HOLMES Exactly. Yet a few moments ago we heard a hansom enter this area and stop. It is still here, Watson, which means *he* is still here...somewhere.

WATSON The Ripper?

NETLEY *half draws his sword stick from its sheath and, ready for attack, waits.*

During this, **HOLMES** *has seen the window – and now moves to it and:*

HOLMES *(breathes)* Watson.

WATSON *moves to look into the window – and then* **WATSON** *and* **HOLMES** *move away to exit – again purporting to be heading for that unseen door that leads into* **KELLY**'s *bedsitter.*

We light the gauze wall so as to see into the bedsitter: We see a restricted area – in the main, a cot bed and the wall behind it. The impression is of a bloodbath – on the wall behind – and on the blanket that covers a recumbent form.

HOLMES *and* **WATSON** *enter the area and regard the scene with horror. Finally it is* **HOLMES** *who pulls aside the blanket to reveal* **KELLY**'s *body.*

I suggest that this is a dummy, for what we briefly see are the remains of a woman who has been disembowelled, throat cut, nose and most of the flesh of her face cut away, both breasts cut off, and large areas of thigh cut away.

Mercifully we do not see it long because **HOLMES** *drops the blanket back onto it.*

As he does so – **NETLEY** *slams his sword stick back into its sheath – turns and hurries away to exit.*

ACT II, SCENE ONE

HOLMES and WATSON remain, examining the area of the bedsitter – HOLMES picks up and pockets the now empty purse that he gave KELLY.

NETLEY *(offstage)* Come on! Run there, my beauty, run!

We hear Sound Effects of a hansom being whipped up and then racing away at high speed.

HOLMES and WATSON react – turn to exit – and we have nothing else to look at but that pathetic, blanket-shrouded figure on the bed.

HOLMES and WATSON enter (from door area) and we kill the lighting on the gauze wall.

By now the Sound Effects of hansom cab is receding fast into silence.

HOLMES We must find Annie Crooks. She is our last surviving link...

WATSON But to what?

HOLMES God only knows.

He holds up, and regards the purse:

And perhaps the Devil too.

HOLMES and WATSON exit.

Now our lighting changes to suggest another area of the streets of London.

BRADBURY enters to keep an assignation, stops, consults his watch, paces – then ANDERSON enters.

BRADBURY Sir Robert... *(Produces some papers)* I could have just as easily brought these to your office.

ANDERSON I preferred that you did not. I have my reason.

BRADBURY There isn't much I'm afraid...address of his Dieppe studio... *(Hands over a paper)*

ANDERSON My information is that he is no longer there.

BRADBURY *(hands over another paper)* Well, that's a short list of all the people he knows on the Continent. All the people I know he knows. Bit far flung – Rome, Berlin, Prague... would you mind telling me what it's all about, Sir Robert? Old Sickert's a good friend, and I wouldn't want him to think I was letting him down by giving you this...

ANDERSON All I can say is that I – we – are interested in Sickert at this time.

BRADBURY Not the only one.

ANDERSON Eh? What do you mean?

BRADBURY Had a couple turn up at the gallery the other day. They were asking about Walter Sickert too.

ANDERSON Who were they?

BRADBURY *(shrugs)* Man and a woman.

ANDERSON What man?!

BRADBURY I dunno. He was almost...sinister...tall, beaky...and those eyes...reminded me of a hawk I once saw on Bodmin Moor. Yes, just like a hawk.

ANDERSON What did they want?

BRADBURY Like you – Sickert...they mentioned Annie too.

ANDERSON Annie?

BRADBURY Annie Crooks. Pretty little thing Walter used to know.

ANDERSON I see. Well, I am obliged to you for your help.

BRADBURY But I'm obliged to help, aren't I – you being the police, official and all that? Sir Robert.

> **BRADBURY** *moves to exit – and* **ANDERSON**'s *concealed panic becomes more obvious now as he produces a whistle*

ACT II, SCENE ONE

and blows a couple of blasts – and a few seconds later **POLICEMAN** *enters, truncheon drawn, ready for trouble – then, reacting, throwing up a salute.*

POLICEMAN Oh, it's you sir.

ANDERSON *(scribbling a note)* You are to take this to Sir William Gull immediately.

As **ANDERSON** *hurries* **POLICEMAN** *away – they exit.*

Curtain rises on:

HOLMES' *chambers.*

KATE*, holding the purse, paces slowly, watched by* **HOLMES** *and* **WATSON***, until finally she stops, shakes her head and:*

KATE I'm sorry...it imparts nothing to me.

HOLMES The fault is mine, not yours. There were many things I might have taken from that charnel house...but the detective in me resisted disturbing what might be a real clue... I was foolish.

KATE No, Sherlock, dedicated, cautious...but never foolish.

WATSON *(a bit miffed, and a mite jealous:)* Well, that's settled then – you are both of you blameless! It doesn't alter the fact that that poor creature Mary Kelly is dead – and we are no further on to solving this mystery.

HOLMES Agreed. It is still a jigsaw, but I think we have added to the pieces.

WATSON Have we? All I can see is a lot of bits of blue with a portion of cloud on 'em!

HOLMES If we can only find Annie Crooks!

At this moment there is a tap at the door and **MRS HUDSON** *enters.*

MRS HUDSON There's a Sir William Gull to see you, sir.

HOLMES *(surprised)* Show him in.

> **MRS HUDSON** *steps aside and* **GULL** *enters.* **MRS HUDSON** *exits.*

GULL Holmes.

HOLMES Sir William.

GULL It is important I talk with you, Holmes...

> *He glances at* **WATSON** *and* **KATE**.

...a matter of some confidentiality.

HOLMES Certainly.

> *To* **KATE**.

Would you excuse us?

> *Then, seeing how she stares at* **GULL**.

Are you well? Is something wrong?

KATE No.

HOLMES Watson, I am sure that Mrs Mead would be fascinated if you were to take her to your rooms and show her your daguerreotypes of the Afghanistan campaign.

WATSON Be delighted.

> **WATSON** *and* **KATE** *exit,* **KATE** *almost backing away from* **GULL**, *and* **HOLMES** *very aware of her reaction.*

GULL Mrs Mead? The medium?

HOLMES The same.

GULL Anxious for your future, are you, Holmes? Consulting your stars?

HOLMES Whether you believe it or not, her instincts are uncanny.

GULL *(thoughtful)* Are they now? Helping you is she?

HOLMES She is indispensable to my current investigation. Now, Sir William...?

GULL Really. I have read of her so-called powers, but put little credence in them until now. *(Suddenly grasps* **HOLMES'** *hand)* I greet you well, Brother Holmes.

HOLMES *is a little taken aback. Then, just as suddenly,* **GULL** *paces away.*

These are troubled times.

HOLMES For a Queen's Physician? For a Knight Commander of the Empire?

GULL I was generalising.

HOLMES Trouble rarely generalises, Sir William. In my experience it is specific – attacking the soft underbelly... of the poor usually.

It is **GULL***'s turn to be taken aback.*

Never mind. You are not here to borrow money then?

GULL Borrow money...? Whatever gave you such an idea?!

HOLMES Then why are you here? I regard a bush as something to decorate a garden, not to be beaten around!

GULL I find your manner offensive, sir.

HOLMES My manner is that of a man preoccupied with other, more pressing problems, but if you find offence in it, then I readily apologise.

GULL The fact is, Holmes, that, as a fellow member of your lodge, as a brother, I am concerned – as indeed are others, that you continue to pursue an investigation that you were warned against.

HOLMES An investigation?

GULL Into the Whitechapel murders.

HOLMES The Whitechapel murders? Can you not bring yourself to say Ripper?! Sir William, you are the second to claim brotherhood and then warn me off! Why? Why should this concern the honourable society to which we both belong?

GULL You cannot be unaware as to how these murders are being politically manipulated? The outcry that is being whipped up for social reform? The filthy rumours that abound...?

HOLMES To my mind the social reforms are long overdue – and the way, the only way, to scotch these "filthy rumours" is to solve the crimes and speedily bring the perpetrator to book! Justice is the eternal cleanser, Sir William.

GULL *regards him for a moment, then:*

GULL And which would you put first; justice as you see it? Or the defence of the Monarchy?

HOLMES They are indivisible surely? It will be a sad day when one cannot survive without the other.

GULL You intend to continue then?

HOLMES I intend to continue with what I have been doing for these many years now; taking a lively interest in, and pitting my wits against, apparently insoluble crime.

GULL Where does your duty lie, man!

HOLMES My duty and my conscience lie here, within my breast – amiable companions, and so far neither has wrestled for ascendancy over the other.

GULL You should be warned, Holmes...

HOLMES *(interjects)* Correction, Sir William, I *have* been warned – and that serves only to intrigue me, to strengthen my resolve.

GULL I bid you good day then.

HOLMES *(a mocking little bow)* Sir William...

He moves to hold the door for him, and then:

ACT II, SCENE ONE

Have you ever performed a lobotomy?

This stops GULL *dead.*

The subject has arisen on another, different case I have been working on, and if I might come to you for some expert, *first hand* advice...?

GULL Yes, I have performed them.

HOLMES Then perhaps we will meet again in the near future.

GULL *exits.* HOLMES *moves away to the window to gaze out.*

A moment – and then WATSON *and* KATE *enter again.*

WATSON Didn't get around to my daguerreotypes. Mrs Mead spied my collection of lepidoptera and found them quite delightful...

KATE Such luminous colours...

HOLMES *(staring off)* An inherited collection, I'm glad to say.

WATSON *and* KATE *are taken aback, they exchange a look.*

If Watson were the sort of man to take something as lovely as a butterfly and then impale it to a board, he would be no friend of mine. Watson.

Without turning, he gestures that WATSON *join him at the window.* WATSON *does, and* HOLMES *points down and off.*

Sir William's coachman. Is there not something familiar about him?

WATSON Eh? Why, yes! It's that Netley fellow, isn't it?

HOLMES *(nods)* That Netley fellow.

We hear Sound Effects of the now familiar sound of a hansom cab starting up and driving off as:

Driving off in a hansom. Shining the seat of his trousers.

WATSON *(to* **KATE***)* He is the man who barged in here and took Devane away!

HOLMES Exactly what Kelly said of Annie Crooks, "they came and took her away".

He turns to regard **KATE**.

Something about Sir William disturbs you?

KATE Yes. I... I don't know what... *(Blurts)* but he frightens me!

WATSON I say, Holmes, you are surely not suggesting that there is any way that Sir William Gull can be involved in...

HOLMES *(overrides)* You know as much as I, Watson, or as little. But of one thing I am certain, somehow Annie Crooks is the key. Which is why we must go to her.

WATSON But we don't know where she is. Do we?

HOLMES They took her away – just as they took Charles Devane away...to...where?

WATSON The St. Giles' Hospice!

HOLMES It is very likely. And this time – with you exerting your medical status, I *will* get beyond the front door!

HOLMES *and* **WATSON** *make ready to leave –* **KATE** *picks up her cape.*

No, not you, you look desperately tired.

KATE Oh, but I...

HOLMES *(overrides)* I would rather you remain here. Mrs Hudson will make you some tea.

KATE Very well.

HOLMES Come, Watson...

As they move to the door:

WATSON *(sotto voce)* Shouldn't ever tell a woman she looks tired, Holmes, it isn't done.

HOLMES You are a positive font of good advice, my dear Watson.

> **HOLMES** *and* **WATSON** *exit.* **KATE** *paces over to the window, looks out, and then, starting to "see" – to sense something, she turns, then eventually covers her face with her hands – concentrating intently then suddenly she takes her hands away, and we see her distraught face as:*

KATE He will need all his strength...all his strength.

Blackout.

Then, during the blackout, we start to creep in Sound Effects of asylum (as used in Act One), building up – up – and then we illuminate **HOLMES**, *standing alone in the asylum.*

***Note**: We can either stage – as with the pub earlier – with only the protagonists and sound and darkness setting the scene. Or, even better, we keep the stage in darkness – save for lights on our principals as required – but, in the gloom we detect writhing, tousled haired, filthy clothed inmates – using those of our players who can be spared for this occasion. It is a women's ward, but if some of our "women" are played by bewigged men, that will only serve to make them look more like mad harridans. The impression is of Hell on Earth!*

HOLMES *remains, the Sound Effects very loud as he looks around him in horror, desperately affected by the scene. Finally, in what is an "internal" speech:*

HOLMES I should have flouted convention, faced your husband and told him of our love... Dear God, is this how you died, in a place like this... Did I condemn you to this?!

WATSON *enters the lit area.*

WATSON Holmes.

He reacts as he sees **HOLMES'** *anguished face.*

Holmes...? Old chap, are you all right? Annie Crooks is here, but we must hurry, she is very ill and sinking fast.

WATSON *leads* **HOLMES** *across the area – and, if we have peopled the shadows with inmates,* **HOLMES** *will be aware of them as he moves past. As they go we should bring down or lose altogether the asylum Sound Effects so that it does not vie with the scene to come. But even if we do not have inmates – every so often, at a salient moment, we may hear an inmate scream, cry out, or moan.*

Illuminate **ANNIE CROOKS**. *She lies on an old mattress, propped up by pillows, covered by blankets – and all of them filthy and torn. In her arms she holds a filthy bundle of rags, crushing it close to her breast. She too is ragged and filthy – her hair wild and matted.* **WATSON** *and* **HOLMES** *enter the area to regard her.*

HOLMES *(horrified)* Have they no water here? Do they not wash and clothe them?!

WATSON I know, place is a disgrace. I intend reporting it to the highest authority.

HOLMES *(very gently)* Annie? Annie Crooks?

ANNIE *shows no reaction at all, she just hums a tuneless repetitive little sound – her poor attempt at a song. She rocks to and fro.*

Does she hear me?

WATSON Impossible to say. They tell me she hasn't responded or spoken in months.

HOLMES Annie. We are your friends, here to help you. Mary sent us. Do you remember Mary? Mary Kelly?

ACT II, SCENE ONE

ANNIE does not look up, but she stops rocking and singing for a moment, then almost immediately continues again. This time the "song" is mixed up with the Latin of a Catholic litany, bowdlerised to become a song.

I struck a note somewhere in that poor brain. Annie! Look at me, Annie.

HOLMES *takes her face and lifts it to his, then reacts as he sees scar on her forehead.*

Do they brutalise them too?!

WATSON Eh?

HOLMES See that scar on her forehead. By God, Watson, I mean to find out who is responsible and...

He is up on his feet, clutching his sword stick...

WATSON No, it's a surgical scar. See how neat it is...

HOLMES Surgical... *(Then)* A lobotomy?

WATSON I would say so, yes.

HOLMES *(softly)* Infamy permeates this whole affair like a plague sickness. What maelstrom of death and deceit are we caught up in, Watson? Whatever it may be, the secret of it is in what they have left of her brain, of that I am sure.

Then, to **ANNIE***:*

Mary Kelly. You knew her in happier times – at your wedding.

ANNIE *stops rocking, and stares at him.*

Do you remember that?

ANNIE *just stares at him.*

And Eddy was there too...

ANNIE*'s reaction is profound, suddenly animated and clutching at* **HOLMES***' arm.*

ANNIE Eddy. Eddy.

HOLMES Now we are getting somewhere! Yes, Eddy...

ANNIE Eddy...loves me.

HOLMES Indeed he does, but tell me more about Eddy.

ANNIE Eddy loves me. Eddy loves me.

HOLMES Tell me about him.

ANNIE *(suddenly fearful)* Mustn't tell. They'll come and take me away. They'll take me away and hurt me...

HOLMES No one will harm you ever again, I'll see to that...tell me about Eddy.

ANNIE No. Mustn't tell...mustn't tell...

HOLMES *(exasperated, to* **WATSON***:)* In heaven's name, who is this mysterious Eddy?

ANNIE They'll hurt Alice.

> **HOLMES** *and* **WATSON** *react – return their attention to* **ANNIE** *as:*

HOLMES Alice?

WATSON Kelly mentioned her.

HOLMES Who is Alice?

ANNIE They wanted to take her away but...

She cackles craftily.

I hid her...hid her...

HOLMES Hid her where? Annie...?

> **HOLMES** *reaches to touch her – but she thinks he is trying to take her bundle – she yells out, jerks it away from him and in so doing she drops the bundle.*

ANNIE No. No...

HOLMES *picks up bundle –* **ANNIE** *still screaming and trying to crawl over, hands outstretched, but she is very weak.*

No…

As **HOLMES** *picks up bundle, it unwraps and from it slips a pathetic, battered doll.*

Alice…Alice…!

HOLMES *hands her back bundle and doll – and she instantly wraps it up, cradles it, croons to it.*

I won't let them take you Alice, mummy's got you…mummy's got you.

HOLMES *and* **WATSON** *stand back – regarding her, then each other.*

HOLMES Alice.

WATSON A child!

HOLMES The progeny of this unfortunate girl – and the mysterious "Eddy". And Sickert left the country carrying a teddy bear. It is beginning to make sense now.

WATSON Not to me it isn't!

HOLMES They are just shadows in my mind at the moment, Watson – shadows starting to take shape and substance. I shall need to smoke a pipe or two on it.

ANNIE *suddenly arches up and screams a spine chilling scream, that quickly becomes a rattling sound deep in her throat – and then she slumps back and is still.*

WATSON *and* **HOLMES** *crouch beside her.*

WATSON *examines her – then shakes his head, and they slowly get to their feet and regard her.* **HOLMES** *arranges the doll in her arms, covers her with blanket.*

No one can harm her now. *(A rising anger:)* But the harm that was done to her...! We will see to it that she gets a decent burial, Watson.

WATSON Of course.

HOLMES *(looking around)* Far from here. In a country churchyard perhaps, where birds sing and spring flowers grow. *(Then)* Let us be gone from this place!

As **WATSON** *and* **HOLMES** *move across the area, we again illuminate that area where we first found* **HOLMES**. **ANDERSON** *enters to stand there.* **HOLMES** *and* **WATSON** *enter the area.*

HOLMES Sir Robert...! How timely to find you here – there are indignities going on in this inhuman place that require your immediate investigation and...

ANDERSON *(overrides)* Sherlock Holmes, I am arresting you on suspicion of murder.

WATSON What?!

HOLMES Whose murder?

ANDERSON Mary Kelly. You were observed leaving the scene of the crime moments after she was killed.

WATSON What utter nonsense.

ANDERSON You were seen there too.

WATSON Ineffable twaddle! Holmes, you are not going to tolerate this?

ANDERSON If you resist, I have men stationed outside the door.

HOLMES It seems then that we have no alternative.

WATSON Holmes...

HOLMES Come, Watson, the sooner we can examine the charge, the sooner we may refute it.

ANDERSON, WATSON *and* **HOLMES** *exit.*

ACT II, SCENE ONE

Blackout and immediately illuminate:

HOLMES' *chambers.*

KATE *is at the window, while* **MRS HUDSON** *lays out tea things – all the while glancing at* **KATE**, *summoning up courage to speak to her.*

MRS HUDSON There, madam.

KATE Thank you, Mrs Hudson.

She returns to the table.

MRS HUDSON The tea cakes I made myself.

KATE Then I am sure they are delicious.

MRS HUDSON It was a recipe my sister taught me.

KATE Oh?

Then, taking the plunge, **MRS HUDSON** *produces a locket on a chain from her apron and dangles it.*

MRS HUDSON This belonged to her. She died last summer.

KATE Oh, I am sorry.

MRS HUDSON Abroad, she was, in India. I hadn't seen her in three years and, of course, I couldn't be there when it happened. I'd rest much easier if I knew she was all right.

KATE *stares at her.* **MRS HUDSON** *extends the locket to her.*

You can do that, can't you, Madam?

A moment, and then **KATE** *takes the locket.*

KATE I can try.

MRS HUDSON Oh, thank you, madam, I would rest much easier.

KATE *clenches locket and chain in her hand and then puts her fist to her forehead, closes her eyes and concentrates.*

A few moments and then:

KATE Her name was... Alice?

MRS HUDSON Yes!

KATE I sense laughter.

MRS HUDSON Oh, she loved a good laugh, did Alice.

KATE And...great calm...contentment.

Then she opens her eyes and:

I'm sorry, that is all.

MRS HUDSON Calm and contented? That's enough for me! Oh, thank you, madam, thank you...

KATE *(suddenly)* And danger.

MRS HUDSON What?!

KATE Danger... Holmes! He is in trouble!

At this moment we hear the door bell offstage.

MRS HUDSON Ooo, Madam, what will we do?

KATE I'm not sure.

Door bell rings again.

You had better answer the door.

MRS HUDSON *exits.* **KATE** *moves to pick up one of* **HOLMES'** *pipes and "concentrate" on it.*

MRS HUDSON *enters, clutching a scrap of paper.*

MRS HUDSON It's a message for you from Mr Holmes, Madam.

KATE *takes paper, unfolds it and reads:*

KATE "Come at once to Dutfield's Yard, Whitechapel..." Who brought this?

MRS HUDSON A ragamuffin with no seat to his trousers.

ACT II, SCENE ONE

KATE This was not written by Holmes.

MRS HUDSON *(takes note to scan it)* Perhaps he wasn't able, Madam, you said he was in trouble.

KATE I must go at once.

KATE moves to exit and **MRS HUDSON** *calls after her.*

MRS HUDSON Yes, Ma'am...you'll find cabs aplenty at the corner of the street.

MRS HUDSON *starts to tidy up, then stops, looks furtively around, then sits down and helps herself to tea. Then she looks upwards and:*

Having a good laugh are you? *(Then)* Well, of course you would – with dear old Uncle Charley – he always had us in fits, didn't he?

She bites into a cake – and, muffled, with her mouth full:

Then there's Auntie Fran, and Dad and Mum...

HOLMES *and* **WATSON** *enter.*

WATSON I particularly enjoyed the look on his face when he found he had to release us...stuff and nonsense!

MRS HUDSON *reacts – initially "caught" talking to herself and sitting down to tea – then, the, astonishment at seeing* **HOLMES**... *She gets to her feet and stares at him as:*

What do you think, Mrs Hudson...? Police had the temerity to actually arrest us! US! The great Sherlock Holmes and his well-known aide and colleague...

HOLMES Mrs Hudson, what is the matter?

MRS HUDSON You shouldn't be here, Sir.

WATSON Just what I've been telling you – if it hadn't been for the fact that he tied them in legal knots – with, I might add, more than a little assistance from me...we'd both be behind bars...

HOLMES *(overrides)* What do you mean, I shouldn't be here?

MRS HUDSON Why, she's just gone looking for you.

HOLMES Who has?

MRS HUDSON Mrs Mead.

HOLMES Now why would she do that?

MRS HUDSON Because you sent for her.

HOLMES What?

MRS HUDSON Here's the very note.

She hands **HOLMES** *the note and:*

HOLMES "Come at once to Dutfield's Yard..." I didn't send this!

MRS HUDSON Then who did, sir?

HOLMES Come, Watson, the game's afoot, there's not a moment to lose!

HOLMES *and* **WATSON** *exit –* **MRS HUDSON** *gazes after them, again eyes the tea things, and with a gesture that says "Oh, well" she sits down again.*

Blackout.

Then illuminate East End street area.

Note: *The details of the staging of the ensuing sequence will naturally depend upon this set. I am suggesting that it is a different East End area to that we have seen before, but will probably be a revamping and repositioning of the elements of previous sets in this area. Ideally there should be at least one wooden, rickety ladder leading up and away (perhaps an element included in earlier sets?) and beneath this ladder is a dark and shadowy area.*

It is here that **NETLEY** *stands, so still and so dark – his face masked by a scarf pulled over nose and mouth – that we do not immediately note his presence. Hopefully this does not happen until he moves slightly and light catches the gleam of the wicked, long-bladed knife he holds in readiness.*

Now we hear Sound Effects of a hansom cab approaching and stopping nearby.

MALE VOICE *(offstage)* The Yard's down there, missus.

KATE *(offstage)* Thank you.

A moment later **KATE** *enters the area – and is placed furthest from* **NETLEY**. *She stops and looks around, then:*

Holmes...?

She moves around the area – getting nearer and nearer to **NETLEY** *until she is within a few feet of him, and with her back turned to him.*

NETLEY, *knife poised, starts to creep out behind her – but then ducks back as a* **POLICEMAN** *enters the area to shine his torch on* **KATE**.

POLICEMAN What are you doing here?

KATE Waiting for a friend.

POLICEMAN Not a good place to wait, not these days. Or any day come to that. Will your friend be long?

KATE I hope not.

POLICEMAN Well, it's a free country, I can't stop you, but I *have* warned you.

POLICEMAN *moves on to exit.*

KATE *remains, pacing fretfully, and then* **NETLEY** *moves, makes a slight noise and* **KATE** *spins around.*

KATE Holmes...? Is that you...?

> **NETLEY** *presses back –* **KATE** *moves forward and past him – and now he springs out behind her – to encircle her throat with his forearm, and with the knife held aloft, drags her back into the deep shadows beneath the ladder.* **KATE** *manages one faint cry, which is immediately choked off by* **NETLEY** *who pulls her even further back so that now all we can see of their deadly struggle is* **KATE***'s hand, seeking purchase to pull free.*
>
> *A moment – and then:*

HOLMES *(offstage)* This way...

> **HOLMES** *and* **WATSON** *enter the area – to stop and look around.*

Kate! Kate!

> *We see* **KATE***'s hand making an imploring gesture, but* **HOLMES** *does not.*

She must be here.

WATSON Perhaps...further down the alley there...

> **WATSON** *and* **HOLMES** *start to move off in a direction away from* **KATE***. They are almost offstage when suddenly something impels* **HOLMES** *to turn about – and now he sees the hand.*

HOLMES Watson!

> *Lifting his stick, he rushes towards the dark area, and even as he does so, so* **NETLEY** *thrusts* **KATE** *out and away, and against* **HOLMES***, impeding him long enough for* **NETLEY** *to slash him across the arm with his knife.* **HOLMES** *steps back, clutching his arm and – Make Up Effects – blood showing under his hand.*
>
> **NETLEY** *runs to start to climb the ladder.*

ACT II, SCENE ONE

WATSON *runs after him, grabs at his feet – but* **NETLEY** *kicks out and catches* **WATSON**, *knocking him down and away.*

NETLEY *exits up the ladder.* **WATSON** *gets to his feet, pulls out his revolver – and starts up the ladder to exit after* **NETLEY**.

HOLMES *has moved to lift and support* **KATE** *who has fallen to the ground, gasping for breath.*

Kate...are you all right? Did he harm you?

KATE   It was terrifying...but I'm shaken, that's all... Oh, Sherlock...

And, starting to tremble violently, she clings to him, then reacts:

But *you* are hurt...!

HOLMES   I'll live.

He flexes his injured arm and, with a rare smile:

And much to Watson's annoyance, I'll probably play the violin again.

The smile fades as he regards her with great affection:

Kate...for a moment I thought I had lost you.

He holds her close – and now Sound Effects – we hear blast of police whistle offstage.

Watson's out there alone!

KATE   You must go to him.

He hesitates.

Go! I'll be safe, he won't dare to return now.

HOLMES *gets to his feet – but at this moment* WATSON *enters, looking a bit crestfallen.*

HOLMES He gave you the slip?

WATSON I almost had him...

POLICEMAN *enters behind* WATSON.

But then this bungling idiot intervened – and, to make matters worse, has insisted upon arresting me! Really, Holmes, twice in one day is enough!

POLICEMAN *(reacts)* Holmes? Mr Sherlock Holmes, is it? Yes, sir, I recognise you. So you, sir, must be Doctor Watson?

WATSON You dullard, that's what I've been trying to tell you.

POLICEMAN I'm sorry, sir.

WATSON Sorry?! I almost had the Ripper in my grasp, and then you...! I shall write a letter to *The Times*. I haven't just heard the first cuckoo I've met him! I say, Holmes, better let me take a look at that wound.

HOLMES It will keep until later. Did you see his face?

WATSON No, fellow was all muffled up. But I was *that* close.

HOLMES Where did you lose him?

WATSON Over that way, by the church, and Holmes... I *thought* I heard a hansom rattle away. Be deuced convenient for him if it was...

HOLMES No. His accomplice was waiting for him.

KATE Accomplice?

POLICEMAN This chap wasn't the Ripper then? Well, there's only one Ripper, isn't there?

HOLMES On the contrary, there are at least two!

WATSON *and* KATE *react.*

Come.

ACT II, SCENE ONE

HOLMES *leads* WATSON *and* KATE *away to exit, leaving the* POLICEMAN *gawping after them.*

Then a STREETWALKER *enters. (**Production note**: she will be played either by the artiste who has played* EDDOWES *and* CROOKS *– or by the additional actress mooted by the director).*

POLICEMAN *pushes back into the shadows. She moves past, then he steps out, and she reacts with a cry.*

STREETWALKER Oooh, you gave me a start. Palpitating I am, palpitating! *(Then)* Show us your badge.

POLICEMAN Eh?

STREETWALKER They say *he* might be dressed as a copper. Show us your badge!

POLICEMAN You gone barmy, Maisie? I've been pounding this beat the past twelve month. I've pulled you in least half a dozen times.

STREETWALKER Well, it don't do not to be careful. Not these days. *(Then, seeing his big grin)* Here, you're looking a bit chipper, pleased with yourself... *(Sudden thought)* Have they caught him? Is that it – they've grabbed him at last?

POLICEMAN *(enjoying his moment)* Not yet, and it's not *him*, Maisie. It's *them*.

STREETWALKER What?

POLICEMAN The Ripper. I've got it on the best authority – there's more than one. At least.

He strolls away to exit. STREETWALKER *remains, stunned, then she looks around, suddenly realising she is alone in the area.*

STREETWALKER Oh my gawd!

We illuminate HOLMES' *rooms.*

KATE is alone, touching her throat, and then HOLMES and WATSON enter (from bathroom area). HOLMES carries his jacket and his shirt sleeve is rolled up to reveal a bandage (which should be set during intermission).

WATSON That's fixed that. Now then, let me have a look at that pretty throat of yours. Hurt, does it?

KATE Not really.

WATSON *(checking her throat)* Well it will, like the very devi... *(Corrects)* ...be very sore indeed, *and* you are going to have a dandy bruise.

KATE I'll just have to wear a scarf.

WATSON You're a very courageous woman, ma'am. Any trouble swallowing?

KATE No.

WATSON No huskiness in the voice either. No irrepairable damage.

HOLMES Thank God.

They look at him as he finishes putting his jacket back on, and wincing slightly as he grips his injured arm, sits gratefully in a chair, with his pipe, etc.

Oh, my faithful and reliable Watson, what would we do without you?

WATSON *(embarrassed)* What are friends for?

HOLMES Indeed. And you are the very best a man might have.

WATSON *(even more embarrassed)* Oh, come along...

And, glad to change the subject with a sudden announcement:

I prescribe a large brandy for you. And an even larger one for me! And for you, dear lady...a cordial.

ACT II, SCENE ONE

As he fixes the drinks:

Holmes, I know your taste for the dramatic, but you really have had long enough.

HOLMES *looks puzzled.*

Keeping us in suspense. *Two* Rippers.

KATE Yes, Sherlock, I am intrigued too.

HOLMES *starts to fill his pipe from the old Persian slipper that serves as humidor, and will light and puff it as:*

HOLMES It begins with you, Kate. When you came to me and urged me to return here to meet a man you said it was "important" – "desperately urgent", and you were right because that man – known to us as Charles Devane – is the pivot to everything. Without him, six unhappy women would still be alive today. Watson, do you recall how he mentioned the Ripper that night…?

WATSON Well…er…he said something about… "The Ripper stalks the streets".

HOLMES No.

WATSON But I distinctly remember…

HOLMES *(interjects)* Not the *Ripper stalks* the streets – but the *Rippers stalk* the streets. The profound "s". At first I too thought it just a slip of the tongue, but I have come to know otherwise. He knew that the Rippers are plural.

WATSON Devane?

HOLMES Ah, yes, *Devane*. Please be so kind as to hand me the copy of the *Illustrated London News* from my desk.

WATSON, *who by now has handed out the drinks, moves to get the magazine and hand it to* **HOLMES**.

What else do you remember of that night, Watson? Of Devane?

WATSON Well...a fellow in a very bad way.

HOLMES The *detail*, Watson. Let me refresh your memory... He told us that he ran away, and then took an omnibus...

WATSON *interjects, pleased at his recall as:*

WATSON But they put him off because he had no money. *(To* **KATE***)* Said he never carried money.

HOLMES Yes, and you, in your innocence, dear Watson, said... "Just like our dear Queen" – and how very close to the truth you were.

WATSON Huh?!

HOLMES Then later, in a complete change of manner, he complimented us on our cognac, then went on to discuss with me. "Personally we feel that the gratitude of the nation is long overdue". I think they were his exact words. "We" – the Royal "we" and then he extended his hand thus...

HOLMES *extends his hand, down.*

As a King might to a loyal subject. Or a Prince.

KATE Sherlock, you are surely not implying...

HOLMES *(overrides)* A hand as soft as a maiden's – a hand that had never seen work!

WATSON Dammit, Holmes, you are not suggesting that broken down hulk of a man was...

HOLMES *(interjects)* ...of Royal blood. Yes.

WATSON Ridiculous! Poppycock! Holmes, I've long admired your facility to turn the unbelievable into palatable fact... but *this* time...! *(Sudden thought)* Royal blood? The man was a Catholic! *(To* **KATE***)* He broke down into some Latin mumbo jumbo...

HOLMES Watson, you are quite splendid! You have unerringly seized upon the motive for these crimes – or a substantial part of it.

KATE *(catching on)* Annie Crooks...?

HOLMES Annie Crooks, a Catholic who went through a form of marriage...

WATSON *(interjects)* ...with a man named William Gorman. *(Defiantly)* I saw it right there on the certificate – <u>William Gorman</u>.

HOLMES *calmly folds the magazine back to a certain page.*

HOLMES Look at this.

WATSON *takes it – scans it – and* **KATE** *moves to look over his shoulder as:*

WATSON What am I supposed to be looking at?

HOLMES Photograph at the top of the page.

WATSON Prince Albert...?

HOLMES *(interjects)* Albert Victor Christian Edward, Duke of Clarence and Avondale. Known to his intimates as "Eddy".

The word hangs on the air for a moment. Then **HOLMES** *fiercely bears in:*

Think of Charles Devane, hold him in your mind...now look again at Prince Eddy. Strip him of perhaps twenty pounds, hollow his cheeks...hurt and harrass him, add a full beard to the moustache...

A long moment and then a very shaken **WATSON** *looks at* **KATE** *and:*

WATSON It could be.

HOLMES It is, Watson, it is. Prince Eddy, who contracted a secret marriage to a Catholic shop girl...who bore him a child.

WATSON Good God.

HOLMES In this instance, God has not been good. God has been cruel.

Sickert, who is involved in some way, has tried to atone by taking the child away to a place of safety.

KATE The teddy bear.

HOLMES *(nods)* The teddy bear.

KATE If this were to leak to the public...

WATSON *(interjects)* ...and there you have the final motive!

They regard him – he is animated and excited now.

The pieces fit – no bits of blue with cloud now, Watson! And I'll wager that somewhere amongst Prince Eddy's staff there was a man named Gorman.

KATE There was. I recall reading about it. A valet who retired – the Prince made a presentation.

HOLMES And then took his name to try and cover up a marriage which might shake the very foundations of our Monarchy... which could topple the Government!

KATE *(finally)* Sherlock, this is too dangerous.

HOLMES I know it. *(Stands up and paces)* But I will not be dissuaded, I will continue until I have brought those responsible to book.

WATSON But who *is* responsible?

HOLMES *paces away, it is a question he does not care to face.*

HOLMES I have a dreadful suspicion. The manner of the killings – "The throat cut across, the breast torn open..."

WATSON Like some ghastly ritual.

ACT II, SCENE ONE

HOLMES *(regards him)* Dear Watson, how intuitive you are. *(Then)* But they are just suspicions – without proof, without fact…I am helpless…

His pacing has taken him to the desk, now he stops dead, staring at it.

What a fool I've been!

And from his desk he takes tip the Ripper letter.

The letter Lestrade lent me. A letter, Kate, in the Ripper's own hand!

She stares at him.

Dear Kate, I know the toll it takes of you, but will you do this for me?

KATE *regards him, and then finally takes the letter from him.*

Draw the curtains, Watson, I will lower the lamp. The dark is the Ripper's domain.

WATSON *draws drapes.* **HOLMES** *moves to adjust lamps – the lights go lower.* **KATE** *holds the letter tentatively, and then moves away across the room – holds the letter to her breast and "concentrates".*

For a few moments she is utterly still, but then she trembles slightly, controls it and then her body attitude becomes more assertive, more masculine as she turns, and in a rasping, almost male voice:

KATE Holmes.

She moves to **HOLMES** *– hand out-stretched. Astonished, he takes it – and then, in a whisper:*

I greet you well.

And she would collapse in a faint – but **WATSON** *and* **HOLMES** *support her and put her into a chair.*

WATSON Water.

He hastens to pour a glass, while **HOLMES** *stands, thunderstruck, looking at his outstretched hand, and then at* **KATE**.

That produced nothing but a dizzy spell.

HOLMES Oh, Watson, if it were only that. She has confirmed what I already knew but did not dare to acknowledge.

WATSON Confirmed? She said nothing and then…she fainted.

HOLMES You know that I belong to a society to which all women are denied?

WATSON Yes.

HOLMES It is impossible. And yet it happened.

WATSON *(tending* **KATE***)* What did?

HOLMES Just now, she did what she could not possibly do… what no woman could ever know. She gave to me the secret handshake of that society!

Then, anxiously bends to her:

Kate…

WATSON Give her some air.

KATE*'s eyes flicker open – she grips her head.*

KATE Did I…?

HOLMES You told me everything.

KATE *Everything*?

HOLMES Everything that I need to know. Will she be all right, Watson…?

WATSON Yes.

HOLMES Are you sure?

WATSON Holmes, you really should acknowledge that I know more about women than you.

HOLMES *(regards* **KATE** *fondly)* I fear that is true. But I am eager to learn.

Then he paces away to pick up his sword stick, cape, etc.

I must go now on a most painful task. I must go alone, and if I should not return...

KATE *(interjects)* Sherlock!

HOLMES *(very firmly)* If I should not return, then you must both of you forget all that we have spoken of in this room tonight.

WATSON But, Holmes...

HOLMES *(overrides)* You must promise me this. I insist upon it.

A moment, and then **WATSON** *nods.*

WATSON Very well.

HOLMES Thank you. Kate?

A moment, and then finally she nods.

I'll not delay then.

He moves to the door, but:

WATSON Holmes!

> **WATSON** *moves to him. They embrace warmly, then* **HOLMES** *turns, regards* **KATE**, *then quickly moves to her, takes her hand, kisses it, then looks at* **WATSON** *who quickly mimes that he should kiss her cheek too!* **HOLMES** *kisses* **KATE**'s *cheek, abruptly turns and moves to exit.*
>
> **WATSON** *and* **KATE** *gaze after him in trepidation.*

Blackout (or curtain?)

Then curtain rises on (or we illuminate:)

A room in GULL's *house. This may be highly stylised; two chairs, a table, a lamp – or may in some way incorporate the Terrace of Act One.*

The Prime Minister, LORD SALISBURY, *and* SIR WILLIAM GULL, *wearing dinner jackets, are enjoying an after dinner brandy and cigar.*

HOLMES *enters and is very charmingly deferential as:*

HOLMES Prime Minister, I greet you well, it is good of you to see me at such short notice, and most appropriate that I find his Lordship enjoying the hospitality of *your* home, Sir William.

SALISBURY I would not normally make myself so readily available, Holmes – but you stressed the urgency of the matter – and when you also made a fraternal appeal...

HOLMES I am grateful.

SALISBURY Now, if you may be quick – the ladies await us.

HOLMES May I ask if Sir William was present when you were first made aware of Prince Eddy's marriage to Annie Crooks?

The question is lightly put, but SALISBURY's *reaction is profound.*

SALISBURY How did you...? Who told you of this...? Gull, the door...?

GULL Is firmly closed.

SALISBURY Holmes, I don't know how you came by this ugly, unfounded rumour, but I must insist that you never again repeat...

ACT II, SCENE ONE

HOLMES *(interjects)* No rumour, Prime Minister. Ugly, yes, I grant you there is much that is ugly about this affair...but I must insist that you answer my question.

SALISBURY *stares at him.*

No matter, your face provides my answer. So, Sir William Gull *was* present – and tell me, Prime Minister....did you, in your anger...in your panic...say something akin to Henry the Second's outburst against Beckett:

"Who will rid me of this troublesome priest?" *"Who will rid me of these troublesome whores"?* Friends of Mary Kelly who was witness to the wedding and who, in turn, made them privy to it?!

GULL This is outrageous...

HOLMES *(calmly overrides)* I would use stronger words, Sir William. Outrageous, yes...but also inhuman, sadistic, barbaric, unspeakably bloody! And the blood is on your hands!

SALISBURY Holmes, you will explain yourself or I will send for my bodyguards and...

HOLMES I *will* explain myself, sir. Nor will I leave here, or be dragged from here until I do...because I cannot, *will not*, believe that you, the political leader of this glorious country of ours, were privy to these abominations.

Regards GULL:

Abominations perpetrated in the name of that pure and noble society to which all in this room belong – and by so doing contaminated it – bringing it to the brink of disgrace and destruction! The rotten apple – poised over the sweet, unblemished fruit...

SALISBURY Holmes!

He stops short as HOLMES *makes a secret sign.*

HOLMES Fidelity. Fidelity. Fidelity.

At **GULL**:

"And the ju-wes are not the men to be blamed for nothing." I stopped off at your coach house on my way here, Sir William. I was looking for your coachman – a man named Netley I believe. A fellow brother and man of...infinite talents. I did not find him. But I did find a burned out hansom cab. It did not look like an accidental burning, but as though someone had put a torch to it. Amongst the remains I found a scrap of leather seat...with blood upon it. That's how you did it, isn't it...? Lured those poor girls into a hansom... and did for them there. It explains the lack of blood – the ease of escape...

SALISBURY Did what?

HOLMES The Ripper murders!

SALISBURY *looks very shaken.*

HOLMES Gull here, and his coachman Netley – like ghouls in the night...and always the knife, eh, Sir William? The tool of your trade – and your obsession...cold steel – whether it be to rip out a woman's guts or slice away that part of her brain that might threaten your scheme! And all for nothing.

SALISBURY Nothing?

HOLMES Prime Minister, you had it in your power to annul such a marriage. The Royal Marriages Act gives you that power – the Prince was under age – married without the Queen's consent, so it could have been construed as illegal. Annie Crooks could have been quietly resettled elsewhere with her child...the Prince rusticated to some remote part of the Empire...?

Instead, those poor women were butchered...and Annie Crooks...sad, sweet Annie Crooks...to die such an abominable death, her child taken from her, confined to an asylum. And the Prince himself...surely he might have been *persuaded, cajoled*...but to submit him to a lobotomy...?

SALISBURY What? *(He looks from* **HOLMES** *to* **GULL**) The Prince is ill, yes, but from a congenital disease.

HOLMES You have been deceived, Prime Minister, the Prince suffers from madness. Other men's madness.

SALISBURY Sir William, you have said nothing to answer these ridiculous accusations?

GULL Do I need to? You say yourself – "ridiculous" – a fiction... does he have proof of any of it?

SALISBURY Well, Holmes?

HOLMES I would like to question Anderson.

SALISBURY Sir Robert?

HOLMES A fellow Mason, and part of this conspiracy too.

SALISBURY Out of the question.

HOLMES Well then...my proof consists only of scraps, none would satisfy a court of law...

GULL There, you see!

HOLMES *(overrides)* But give me the coachman – Netley. I know the Netleys of this world. Grubbing upstarts, eager to ingratiate and influence and eventually hold sway over their masters. Give me him and I promise you, when his own evil neck is at risk, he will crack.

SALISBURY Is this man here?

GULL You are surely not giving credence to this tissue of lies...?

SALISBURY *(overrides)* Is he here?!

GULL I don't know.

SALISBURY Then perhaps you, Holmes, will go and find out, and summon him?

HOLMES *nods, hurries away to exit.*

Tell me quickly, Sir William, what you know of this...?

GULL Prime Minister...

SALISBURY *(overrides)* Only a madman would make such an accusation, and I do not think Holmes to be mad. Eddy's marriage promised a scandal, but *this*...?! If it were only half true and it were to become public knowledge.

GULL There is no need of that. Only Holmes knows.

SALISBURY Knows what? You have assured me there is nothing *to* know!

GULL Only Holmes is obsessed with his *mad theory, so let's use his madness against him.* (*Warming to his theory*) Have him declared insane. Certified. It can be arranged under my signature, then we could put him away, and perhaps, in a little while, medical prognosis might call for a lobotomy, an operation to remove that part of his brain that threatens us. So simple, so quick and easy... *(Gesticulates)* ...the cleansing knife...!

GULL *suddenly stops, aware of* **SALISBURY**'s *horrified gaze, aware that he has betrayed his insanity. And, fumbling to recoup ground now:*

I'm thinking of our country, of course, of protecting Her Majesty...

HOLMES *enters.*

HOLMES Netley is here and has been sent for. Prime Minister, when he arrives, I beg of you that only *I* be allowed to speak to him.

SALISBURY *(still staring at* **GULL***)* Yes, Holmes, it shall be exactly as you say.

HOLMES *looks at him, reacting to, and puzzled by, his change in tone and manner.*

Then we hear a tap at a door – and a moment later **NETLEY** *enters, ramrod straight, like a Sergeant Major, with his stick tucked under his arm, hat in hand.*

NETLEY You sent for me, sir...?

HOLMES *(steps forward)* I sent for you.

NETLEY *recognises* **HOLMES**, *is a bit taken aback, and quickly looks to* **GULL**.

GULL Netley, do not...

SALISBURY *(overrides)* Sir William!

GULL, *silenced, steps back,* **HOLMES** *advances on* **NETLEY**, *rubbing his recently injured arm.*

HOLMES The game's up, Netley. Sir William has told us how you carried out the Ripper killings...

NETLEY How *I* did...?! It was him. I just drove the coach...

GULL *(simultaneously)* Netley... No...

HOLMES *(overrides)* He's thrown you to the wolves...and I am now arresting you for the murder of...

NETLEY No!

NETLEY *steps back, drawing his sword stick.*

Stay back. Out of my way...!

He is moving to exit, but suddenly **HOLMES** *draws his sword stick and moves to bar his way.*

And they fight an exciting duel – to and fro – a duel that culminates when **NETLEY** *lunges in with a death thrust, and* **HOLMES**' *brilliantly parries it and runs* **NETLEY** *through.* **NETLEY** *falls to the ground to lie still.*

A frozen moment and then:

SALISBURY My God. What have I done?!

HOLMES It is now a question of what you can *do*, Lord Salisbury, to make amends...*and guarantee my silence.*

SALISBURY Yes. Yes.

HOLMES The child – Alice must never be sought. She must be left alone to live out her life in peace...

SALISBURY Whatever you say...

HOLMES Anderson will be quietly retired from public life.

SALISBURY Agreed.

HOLMES (*regards* **NETLEY**) This man, should he survive his wound...I never want to see again.

SALISBURY *wearily nods.* **HOLMES** *finally turns to regard* **GULL**.

And as for *him*...he should be taken from here, committed, and confined in an asylum for the insane.

GULL *recoils as though struck.*

A moment – and then blackout.

Then illuminate:

HOLMES' *chambers.*

MRS HUDSON *bustles around, holding a small carpet bag into which she drops a couple of pipes, some tobacco, and then, as an afterthought,* **HOLMES'** *violin case. Then, on another afterthought, she takes it out again as:*

MRS HUDSON She won't want to be doing with that!

WATSON *enters.*

WATSON I say, Mrs Hudson, what's going on?

MRS HUDSON I'm helping Mr Holmes to pack, sir.

WATSON Pack? Why – where's he off to?

ACT II, SCENE ONE

HOLMES *enters from through door leading to bathroom/ bedroom. He carries a valise.*

HOLMES Europe.

WATSON Really? Bit swift, isn't it? I didn't know you had a trip planned.

HOLMES I didn't know she would come.

WATSON She?

HOLMES Kate. Mrs Mead. She has agreed to accompany me, properly chaperoned of course. She has a daughter whom I am hoping to get to know a great deal better.

WATSON Just the two of you, eh?

HOLMES The *three* of us, Watson.

Then, gently:

I did intend telling you, old fellow.

WATSON Well…rest will do you good – certainly deserve one.

HOLMES I'm inclined to agree.

WATSON And while you're away, I can begin that memoir of your work I've always promised to embark on.

HOLMES Capital.

WATSON I'd like to start with the Ripper Murders.

HOLMES *pauses, regards him.*

Trouble is, you haven't confided the full details to me yet.

HOLMES And I never shall. Fidelity! Believe me, Watson, it is for the sake of many.

During this, **KATE** *enters.*

My dear Kate. Commendably punctual, I like that in a woman.

Consults his watch:

We now have plenty of time to catch the boat train... Mrs Hudson. Watson.

WATSON Where shall I reach you...?

HOLMES You won't. I plan this to be a proper holiday.

KATE Oh, but we will send you a postal card from time to time...

KATE *kisses* **WATSON** *on the cheek.*

HOLMES Indeed we shall, and the first from Switzerland. I—

He looks fondly at **KATE***:*

we – are seeking peace and tranquility amongst the mountains...

KATE And you have promised to show me the, Reichenbach Falls...

HOLMES Indeed I did. And I shall. You will love it, Kate – such a beautiful and untroubled spot...

As **HOLMES** *and* **KATE** *exit.*

Final curtain.

FURNITURE AND PROPERTY LIST

ACT I

P2 – Lamplighter's pole.
P2 – Small bottle of liqueur/handbag - Eddowes.
P3 – Bottle of gin.
P6 – Hypodermic needle in a small box/tourniquet.
P8 – Cigar/cigar case – Sir Anderson.
P12 – Policeman's whistle on chain. Bloodied garment – Eddowes.
P12 – *The Times* newspaper.
P13 – Ashtray and cigar remains.
P14 – Doorbell.
P14 – Bandages to cover Eddy's head (professional bandaging).
P16 – Decanter of brandy & gin. Four brandy glasses.
P17 – Revolver.
P19 – Large gentleman's handkerchief.
P19 – Watch on a chain – Watson.
P26 – Document.
P28 – Piece of paper.
P30 – Letter. Piece of paper to hold letter.
P30 – Tray of breakfast things for two.
P30 – Hand towel.
P36 – Brooch of entwined serpents in a box.
P38 – Few paintings on easels, one with a note on back. Unframed painting.
P40 – Tray of tea things, delicate, best china for three.
P42 – Copy of certificate of marriage.

ACT II

P52 – Beggar's tray of matches. Match to light a very bright, large flame.
P53 – Coin.
P55 – Money – one note.
P57 – Pistol – Watson.
P57 – Blind beggar's cane.
P58 – Policeman's lantern.
P59 – Hip flask.
P59 – Purse of twenty guineas.

P64 – Sword stick – Holmes.
P66 – Kelly's body, disemboweled. Blanket.
P66 – Sword stick – Netley.
P67 – Empty purse.
P67 – Pocket watch – Bradbury.
P67 – Papers.
P68 – Police whistle – Anderson.
P69 – Notebook and pencil – Anderson.
P76 – Asylum bed/bedding.
P76 – Bundle of rags with doll inside.
P81 – Tea things for three, including tea cakes.
P81 – Locket on chain.
P82 – Holmes' pipe.
P82 – Folded paper with message.
P85 – Long-bladed knife.
P86 – Bloodied handkerchief/sleeve – Holmes.
P86 – Arm bandage – Holmes.
P90 – Two brandies, one cordial.
P91 – Pipe and tobacco in a pouch.
P91 – Copy of *The Illustrated London News*.
P95 – Lamp in Holmes' room.
P96 – Jug of water & glass.
P98 – Two glasses of brandy, cigars.
P104 – Carpet bag/luggage.
P104 – Violin case.
P105 – Valise.

THIS IS NOT THE END

Visit samuelfrench.co.uk and discover the best theatre bookshop on the internet

A vast range of plays
Acting and theatre books
Gifts

samuelfrench.co.uk

samuelfrenchltd

samuel french uk